Mentoring

Make it a mutually rewarding experience

Fourth Edition

Gordon F. Shea
Stephen C. Gianotti

A Crisp Fifty-Minute™ Series Book

AXZO PRESS

Mentoring

Make it a mutually rewarding experience

Fourth Edition

Gordon F. Shea
Stephen C. Gianotti

CREDITS:

President, Axzo Press:	**Jon Winder**
Vice President, Product Development:	**Charles G. Blum**
Vice President, Operations:	**Josh Pincus**
Director, Publishing Systems Development:	**Dan Quackenbush**
Copy Editor:	**Catherine M. Albano**

Trademarks

Crisp Fifty-Minute Series is a trademark of Axzo Press.

Some of the product names and company names used in this book have been used for identification purposes only and may be trademarks or registered trademarks of their respective manufacturers and sellers.

Disclaimer

We reserve the right to revise this publication and make changes from time to time in its content without notice.

ISBN 10: 1-4260-1838-X
ISBN 13: 978-1-4260-1838-1
Printed in the United States of America
1 2 3 4 5 6 7 8 9 10 12 11 10 09

Table of Contents

About the Author

Gordon F. Shea is the author of 15 books and over 200 articles on subjects such as organizational development, leadership/management, communications, team building, and workforce development. He enjoys an active consulting and training practice in those subjects.

Mr. Shea has authored a companion Crisp *Fifty-Minute* book for mentees titled *Making the Most of Being Mentored.* He has published dozens of articles on mentoring in such periodicals as the *Managing Diversity Newsletter, Supervision, Women in Computing, Bottom Line Business,* and the *Commandant's Bulletin* (U.S. Coast Guard).

Mr. Shea and Crisp Publications have also collaborated on creating a bestselling training video, *Mentoring,* which demonstrates both sides of the relationship.

Mr. Shea's Management Briefing book, *Mentoring: Helping Employees Reach Their Full Potential,* was published by the American Management Association for their membership list. This work was subsequently revised and expanded for publication by Crisp.

Preface

This book provides a solid foundation for understanding the concept of and developing successful behaviors for a mentoring relationship. It enables the reader to identify and assess his or her own mentoring opportunities and experiences—as mentor or mentee—and to use mentoring as an empowering tool for positive professional and personal development.

The book deals with the practical aspects of mentoring, such as what makes mentoring so unique and such a powerful tool, assessing what the mentor is able and willing to invest in the relationship, and the special opportunities and challenges of cross-cultural, cross-gender, and supervisor-employee mentoring.

These how-to sections of the book deal with understanding the needs in a mentoring relationship, positive mentor behaviors, behaviors that can prove to be problematic, and ways to make the most of the mentor/mentee relationship in the short and long run.

This publication can be used as an individual workbook for understanding and exploring mentoring, or as a series of exercises to supplement a course on mentoring. Many of the exercises provide a basis for classroom or small-group discussion as well as personal reflection.

Additionally, the 50-item, multiple-choice and true/false questionnaire will provide you helpful practice in reflecting on your learning and will challenge you to fully gain the knowledge that lies between these covers.

I wish you the best of luck in your learning and, more importantly, may you realize success in each and every mentoring experience that you participate in. Each one can change a life and can play a role in changing an organization.

Stephen C. Gianotti,
Co-author

Learning Objectives

Complete this book, and you'll know how to:

1) Discuss mentoring from its historical beginning to its multiple applications in current use.

2) Use mentoring to play an important role in the development of other people.

3) Create, maintain, and transition a mentoring relationship.

4) Provide specific behaviors to adopt or stay away from to maximize the impact of a mentoring relationship.

5) Use mentoring to improve today's workplace.

Workplace and Management Competencies mapping

For over 30 years, business and industry has utilized competency models to select employees. The trend to use competency-based approaches in education and training, assessment, and development of workers has experienced a more recent emergence within the Employment and Training Administration (ETA), a division of the United States Department of Labor.

The ETA's General Competency Model Framework spans a wide array of competencies from the more basic competencies, such as reading and writing, to more advanced occupation-specific competencies. The Crisp Series finds its home in what the ETA refers to as the Workplace Competencies and the Management Competencies.

Mentoring covers information vital to mastering the following competencies:

Workplace Competencies:

▶ Teamwork

Management Competencies:

▶ Supporting Others

▶ Developing & Mentoring

For a comprehensive mapping of Crisp Series titles to the Workplace and Management competencies, visit www.CrispSeries.com.

About the Crisp 50-Minute Series

The Crisp 50-Minute Series was designed to cover critical business and professional development topics in the shortest possible time. Our easy-to-read, easy-to-understand format can be used for self-study or for classroom training. With a wealth of hands-on exercises, the 50-Minute books keep you engaged and help you retain critical skills.

What You Need to Know

We designed the Crisp 50-Minute Series to be as self-explanatory as possible. But there are a few things you should know before you begin the book.

Exercises

Exercises look like this:

EXERCISE TITLE

Questions and other information would be here.

Keep a pencil handy. Any time you see an exercise, you should try to complete it. If the exercise has specific answers, an answer key will be provided in the appendix. (Some exercises ask you to think about your own opinions or situation; these types of exercises will not have answer keys.)

Forms

A heading like this means that the rest of the page is a form:

FORMHEAD

Forms are meant to be reusable. You might want to make a photocopy of a form before you fill it out, so that you can use it again later.

A Note to Instructors

We've tried to make the Crisp 50-Minute Series books as useful as possible as classroom training manuals. Here are some of the features we provide for instructors:

▶ PowerPoint presentations

▶ Answer keys

▶ Assessments

▶ Customization

PowerPoint Presentations

You can download a PowerPoint presentation for this book from our Web site at www.CrispSeries.com.

Answer keys

If an exercise has specific answers, an answer key will be provided in the appendix. (Some exercises ask you to think about your own opinions or situation; these types of exercises will not have answer keys.)

Assessments

For each 50-Minute Series book, we have developed a 35- to 50-item assessment. The assessment for this book is available at www.CrispSeries.com. *Assessments should not be used in any employee-selection process.*

Customization

Crisp books can be quickly and easily customized to meet your needs—from adding your logo to developing proprietary content. Crisp books are available in print and electronic form. For more information on customization, see www.CrispSeries.com.

What is Mentoring
& Why it Matters

"*What lies behind us and what lies before us are tiny matters compared to what lies within us.*"

–Oliver Wendell Holmes

In this part:

- ▶ The Story of Mentor
- ▶ What Mentors Do
- ▶ The Enabling Mentor
- ▶ Mentoring Today
- ▶ What Does Mentoring Look Like?
- ▶ The Power of Relationships in Our Lives
- ▶ Mentors Care Beyond the Work
- ▶ A Mentor Goes Above and Beyond

The Story of Mentor

The concept of a Mentor originates in Homer's *Odyssey,* written around 8th century BC. When Odysseus leaves for the Trojan War, he entrusts his son Telemachus to a man named Mentor, who serves as his teacher.

A mentor is a trusted teacher or counselor who plays an influential role in a person's life. The person being mentored is called a protégé or a mentee.

Some specific examples of a mentoring relationship include the following:

Mentee	Mentor
Tiger Woods	Bill Walsh (Coach of the 49ers) and Tiger's father, Earl Woods
Alexander the Great	Aristotle
Venus Williams	Pam Shriver
Michelle Obama	Valerie Jarrett (Chicago lawyer and civic leader)

Many films depict the multidimensional nature of a mentoring relationship. Examples include Star *Wars: A New Hope,* as well as the *Karate Kid* and *Lord of the Rings* series. By watching these movies, one can see how both the mentee and the mentor benefit from the relationship.

Mentoring can be a critically important part of human development where one's perspectives and abilities are formed. Mentors often make the critical difference in helping a person to realize potential.

HOW HAS MENTORING BEEN PART OF YOUR LIFE?

The following questions ask about important moments in your life. For this exercise, we are asking you to focus on the developments or changes that occurred within you. How did events change the way you viewed yourself, others, or the world?

1. Who provided an "aha!" experience that changed how you think about yourself, another person, or an event? How did the experience change you?

   _____

   _____

   _____

   _____

2. Who provided you with a quote that influenced your thinking or behavior, and that you sometimes repeat in your head or to others? Write the quote and its significance to you.

   _____

   _____

   _____

3. Who helped you uncover an unrecognized talent or ability? Describe at least one such incident and what difference it has made in your life.

   _____

   _____

   _____

   _____

" *I've learned that people will forget what you said, people will forget what you did, but people will never forget how you made them feel.*"

—Maya Angelou

What Mentors Do

Mentors do many things for an individual. One important thing that they do is enable others. When someone enables another person, they create opportunities. An example might be, "Sally was my mentor. She used her wisdom and experience to instill confidence in me." Sally enabled the person to feel and think differently.

Mentoring styles can vary. A mentor can be a persistent encourager who helps someone build self-confidence or a stern taskmaster who teaches a student to appreciate excellence in performance. Whatever the style, mentors usually care about the mentees and want them to succeed. Often, this caring is the glue of the mentoring relationship.

Effective mentoring can be a powerful force for change because it causes what is known as a *mental model shift*. This is a change in how one thinks or sees things. By thinking differently one is able to behave differently. This is the heart of effective mentoring.

The intent and the result of mentoring are human growth. At work we hope to be more effective at what we are paid to do, and we hope this provides advancement opportunities. In our personal lives, we work toward happy home lives and better relationships with friends and relatives. Effective mentoring can touch every facet of an individual's life.

To gain from mentoring, a mentee has to reach out and draw in the lessons that mentors offer. The mentee can experience the benefits of mentoring by assuming ownership of what the mentor offers and applying it to all aspects of life.

FROM LEGEND TO CHALLENGE

Mentors are people who have a significant impact on our lives. For each item below, write the name of one person who had an influence on you.

Knowledge of organizational systems or processes _____

Values _____

Use of technology _____

Character growth _____

Understanding of how to behave in social situations _____

Understanding of the world _____

Understanding of roles in family dynamics _____

Moral development _____

Mental or physical health _____

Understanding others and their viewpoints _____

Other _____

Mentor: Someone whose hindsight can become your foresight."

–Anonymous

The Enabling Mentor

An effective mentor respects the mentee's uniqueness and strives to enhance that person's special strengths. The best mentors guide and question without judging. This ancient and well-proven method is called the *Socratic Method*. This method teaches by asking questions instead of by instructing or judging.

For example rather than telling a mentee that what s/he did was incorrect, the mentor using the Socratic method might ask, "What were the advantages and disadvantages of doing it that way?" During the discussion the mentee might realize there was a better way.

Effective mentors help the mentee understand the relationship between *what* they do and *how* they do it. Mentors try to focus on the positive results of a transaction. If there are none, the mentor finds ways to end a transaction on a positive note.

Any person can become very attached to the way they do things. Doing something "my way" is critical to some individuals' sense of self. Learning to do a task the mentor's way might lessen the mentee's sense of ownership in the task. However, it can also be a way of avoiding responsibility for the change.

A mentee who is fully invested in the mentoring relationship should adapt the mentor's help to the situation or to personal style. This enables the mentee to wrestle with the details, perhaps by trying different approaches, and discovering personal talents or strengths.

An effective mentor keeps a distance and does not take charge of the mentee. When a mentee feels forced, the mentoring relationship is less effective. Free will is an important aspect of mentoring. This is why being both a mentor and the supervisor or manager can be very tricky. The success of a mentoring relationship hinges on the mentor recognizing and helping to facilitate the mentee's feeling of ownership in the relationship and the tasks at hand. People who have been mentored often recognize that something very special happened, but they may not know what to call the experience.

Mentoring is a process whereby mentor and mentee work together to discover and develop the mentee's latent abilities. The mentor encourages the mentee to acquire knowledge and skills as opportunities and needs arise. The mentor serves as a tutor, counselor, friend, and foil who enables the mentee to sharpen skills and practice critical thinking.

NON-DIRECTIVE WAYS OF MENTORING

Identify three situations in which you served or could serve as a role model.

1. _____
2. _____
3. _____

List two positive attitudes you display, and two ways you help others to overcome negative feelings about themselves.

Positive attitudes:

1. _____
2. _____

Helping others:

1. _____
2. _____

How effective are you at just listening to others' problems?

_____

_____

People seldom want to be told what they should do or how to do it, but an idea offered in a neutral manner becomes something they can identify and use. How would you assess your own ability to share ideas and information in a neutral context without "telling" the person what to do?

_____

_____

Mentoring is a brain to pick, an ear to listen, and a push in the right direction."

–John C. Crosby

WHAT MENTORS DO

Following is a list of some things that mentors do. Check all that apply.

Mentor	Others have done this for me	I've done this for others
1. Set high performance expectations	❑	❑
2. Offer challenging ideas	❑	❑
3. Help build self-confidence	❑	❑
4. Encourage professional behavior	❑	❑
5. Offer friendship	❑	❑
6. Confront negative behaviors and attitudes	❑	❑
7. Listen to personal problems	❑	❑
8. Teach by example	❑	❑
9. Provide growth experiences	❑	❑
10. Offer quotable quotes	❑	❑
11. Explain how the organization works	❑	❑
12. Go beyond duties or obligations	❑	❑
13. Stand by their mentee in critical situations	❑	❑
14. Offer wise counsel	❑	❑
15. Encourage winning behavior	❑	❑
16. Inspire to excellence	❑	❑
17. Share critical knowledge	❑	❑
18. Offer encouragement	❑	❑
19. Assist with careers	❑	❑

> *"We make a living by what we get, we make a life by what we give."*
>
> –Winston Churchill

"Alright, I'll mentor you. How many pushups can you do?"

Mentoring Today

Traditionally, mentoring was a formal process in which an older, more experienced person helped and guided a younger person in learning the ropes within an organization. Mentoring described the activities of a senior person preparing a junior for a particular office or job, providing career guidance, and encouraging high performance standards.

Mentors were senior people in an organization who took talented young people under their wings and protected, taught, and even sponsored them. However, mentoring today has grown beyond its traditional "older helping junior" concept.

There are many reasons why mentoring evolved. First, changing workplace demographics show a broader range of ages, races, backgrounds, disabilities, and education levels. Combined with the advent of virtual working, this has encouraged organizations to rethink how mentoring is done.

Also, traditional mentoring often meant two similar people being involved in the mentoring relationship. Today's mentoring quite literally knows very few boundaries and has been broadened to include mentoring relationships that were not common in the past.

In cross-gender mentoring, a female mentors a male or vice versa. This can be very effective and the best mix of talent, skill, and wisdom for a particular mentoring goal.

Cross-cultural mentoring, like cross-gender mentoring, is quite common today given both the global marketplace and the changed work environment. The more we become familiar with people that are not like us, the broader our understanding of the world and our place in it.

Supervisor or manager mentoring is sometimes done as well. However, a word of caution here: One of the key success factors in a mentoring relationship is the mentee's comfort level in speaking candidly, to express concerns, fears, and hopes. The mentee must be confident that failure when trying something new won't be used in any judgmental way. If a supervisor is a mentor to his/her employee, there is always that power differential. This could prove challenging when problems arise in the non-mentoring portion of their relationship.

For example, if my direct manager is my mentor and she gives me a directive regarding my work, I know I am going to be accountable for the outcome. Ideally my mentor would be a different person that I could go to for advice on that directive. This is not to say that my direct manager can't be a mentor. Boundaries must be clear for these two sometimes conflicting roles.

INSIGHTS ON TODAY'S MENTORING

List some differences between traditional mentoring and mentoring today.

1. _____
2. _____
3. _____

List three potential advantages of cross-gender mentoring:

1. _____
2. _____
3. _____

List three potential advantages of cross-cultural mentoring:

1. _____
2. _____
3. _____

List some potential advantages and disadvantages to being mentored by a direct superior.

1. _____
2. _____
3. _____
4. _____
5. _____

Differences challenge assumptions."

—Anne Wilson Shaef

What Does Mentoring Look Like?

There is really no single answer to this question. Mentoring can take many forms and dimensions. That is partly why it is so powerful and so useful in the workplace. The flexibility in creating mentoring relationships can be quite broad.

Mentoring can occur in a variety of different relationships at any time or place. Mentoring can take the form of a one-shot intervention or a lifelong relationship. It can be carried out informally as an element of friendship, or formally as part of a highly structured employee orientation program.

Mentoring also can happen almost unconsciously. Someone may do or say something that will influence someone else. Or the recipient may become only slowly aware of how important a given intervention has been. It can look like a long-term and highly structured relationship, as in quadrant #2 below. It can be infrequent interaction and relatively short, as in quadrant #3 below. After you have read each quadrant below, think about the various relationships that you have experienced. See if any of them fit into one of these quadrants. If you could change that experience, would you have liked it to have been in a different quadrant? If so, why?

Highly Structured	1. Highly structured, short term	2. Highly structured, long term
	The relationship is formally established for an introductory or short period, often to meet specific organizational objectives. For example, a new employe may be paired with a senior person for company orientation.	Often used for succession planning, this relationship involves grooming someone to take over a departing person's job function, or to master a craft.
	3. Informal, short term	4. Informal, long term
Little Structure	Off-the-cuff mentoring ranges from one-shot spontaneous help to occasional or as-needed counseling. There may be no ongoing relationship. This type of intervention is often heavily change-oriented.	"Friendship mentoring" consists of being available as needed to discuss problems, listen, and share knowledge.

Formality of Relationship

Short-Term Spontaneous ————————————→ Long-Term, Perhaps for Life

Length of Relationship

These empowering links are not just beneficial accidents. Their power springs from the giving nature of the mentor and the receptiveness of the mentee to absorb and use lessons. It's highly likely that many of us will have such experiences in our life, both as mentor and as mentee.

The Power of Relationships in Our Lives

Ernest Hemingway wrote a short story called *The Capital of the World*. Published in 1936, it is the story of a young waiter named Paco and his aspiration to be a matador.

In the story, it was clear that Paco's relationship with his father had broken down. Paco ran away to pursue his dreams. In an effort to rebuild their relationship, his father searched all of Spain hoping to reconnect with his son.

After a long and unsuccessful journey to find his son, Paco's father tried one last time. The father placed an ad in a Madrid newspaper. The ad read:

> *Dear Paco,*
>
> *Meet me in the front of the newspaper office tomorrow at noon.*
>
> *All is forgiven.*
>
> *I love you.*

At noon the next day, hundreds of men named Paco arrived at the newspaper office, each looking to rebuild a relationship that had gone bad.

One moral of this story could be that we should never underestimate the importance of relationships in our lives. This becomes very evident in a mentoring relationship when the mentoring is done well.

As a sad and ironic footnote, Ernest Hemingway died years later from a self-inflicted gunshot wound. One can't help but wonder what kind of difference a mentoring relationship could have meant for him.

SHARING LIFE EXPERIENCE

Write your answers in the spaces provided.

1. Has anyone ever arranged an unusual learning experience for you that allowed you to see into another sphere of life or to look behind the scenes? Describe one such episode.

   _____

   _____

   _____

2. Describe the most unusual mentoring experience you have encountered, and indicate its importance to you.

   _____

   _____

   _____

3. Identify one situation where you provided an unusual experience for another person, which opened new vistas for them, enabled them to see how other people live, or helped them see something important in a new light.

   _____

   _____

   _____

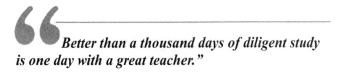

Better than a thousand days of diligent study is one day with a great teacher."

–Japanese proverb

Mentors Care Beyond the Work

Mentoring involves sharing skills and abilities. It also requires big doses of intuition and feelings. Mentors must occasionally make it up as they go along. Learning this is too unstructured for some people, but mentoring is largely organic. Much of mentoring's power is derived from this reality.

Even formal mentoring has an organic aspect. There is an element of emerging property in all mentoring relationships. An *emerging property* is something that comes out of interaction that is not expected or defined in advance. This non-specific and non-concrete element of mentoring can be confusing to those who need a cookbook approach to every task. Individuals who have this need want to know exactly what they are supposed to do, how to do it, and when.

When this need exists, the Mentor must find an approach that is helpful and meets the mentee where s/he is at the time. The mentee must allow him/herself to try something new, different, and possibly less structured. Some of the best learning and most surprising experiences occur when there is no structure.

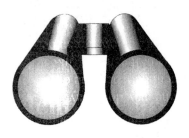

For example, when we travel to a new place, particularly to a different country, we are able to experience something new. Inherent in experiencing new things is that we (can) learn something new as well. This author has frequently found himself lost in a foreign city looking for a specific restaurant, bank, or museum. It was while lost that I experienced some of my most thrilling and memorable experiences.

The same thing is true of mentoring. Some of the best mentoring occurs when we allow it to unfold with little or no "maps" and experience the process of discovering what is found along the way.

This unique element of mentoring reveals new aspects of things in a flash, and is often missing in our other daily activities. Mentors are people who care enough about a person to make this kind of experience happen. Mentoring goes beyond what we learn in day-to-day routine.

Why are today's organizational leaders so interested in promoting a type of relationship that is so amorphous and random? Because in an increasingly complex, high-tech, and global environment we all experience a need for special insight, understanding, and information that is outside the normal channels or training programs. There may be people around us who can provide the missing pieces in our understanding of the complexities that come our way each day. These kinds of people, specifically mentors, care way beyond the work.

IDENTIFYING THOSE WHO CARE BEYOND THE WORK

Identify three people who significantly and beneficially influenced you.
Describe what they contributed to your life:

1. Describe someone who inspired you to shift the direction of your life in a constructive way.

   _____

   _____

   _____

2. Describe someone who helped you grow in depth of feeling, character, or moral or ethical integrity, or who has helped you develop a deeper commitment to your values.

   _____

   _____

   _____

3. Describe someone who provided some form of guidance to you at *just the right time.*

   _____

   _____

   _____

Were any of these assists a spontaneous response to a great need of yours— whether you had recognized the need at the time or not? If so, which?

_____

_____

_____

Keep away from people who try to belittle your ambitions. Small people always do that, but the really great make you feel that you, too, can become great."

—**Mark Twain**

A Mentor Goes Above and Beyond

Except in formal mentoring programs, a mentoring relationship is not duty bound. Mentoring is more than doing a job—it is help that goes beyond an obligatory relationship.

Teachers can mentor and so can lawyers. The difference between a teacher and a great teacher is often due to the extra mentoring component that some people offer. Most of us have known good teachers who do their work with art and style. The fortunate ones among us also have encountered teachers who have fired a spark within us, who opened new vistas and dimensions before us, who touched us deeply, and who awakened and encouraged our potential.

Similarly, a senior lawyer might take a young person fresh from the bar exam under his or her wing. The senior lawyer might teach the novice the ropes of the legal profession, call on the mentee to meet the most exacting professional standards, and provide encouragement during the tough period of getting settled in a law firm.

Mentoring requires going above and beyond. It is a relationship in which a person with greater experience guides another person to develop both personally and professionally to meet exceptional standards of performance.

But what of the senior person in an organization who has been *assigned* the task of mentoring a junior person in a formal mentoring program? If that person performs his duties in a perfunctory fashion, the essence of the experience will be missed for both mentor and mentee.

REACHING OUT TO ANOTHER PERSON

Mentoring is often the extra increment of help that makes a truly important difference to a mentee.

Relate an experience in which you reached out to another person who was deeply in need, and your help appeared to make a significant beneficial and perhaps long-lasting difference to that person.

_____

_____

_____

Describe one experience you observed, read, or heard about in which someone reached out to another person to help in an unusual way. You might remember one that has an imaginative or unusual twist to it that helped make the experience memorable and of continuing utility to the receiver.

_____

_____

_____

Describe one mentoring experience you have had that did not fit the direct, one-on-one personal aspect of mentoring. For example, a special parental message, a quote from literature, a speech, a sermon, and so on.

_____

_____

_____

> *Looking back across my timeline through school, and indeed in the early days of teaching, I see one good thing about being filled with insecurities. Knowing that I had everything to gain, I seemed to seek out mentors."*

—Shirley McPhillips

Part Summary

In this part you learned what mentors **do**, and how they can **influence** one's life. You learned how a mentor **enables** a mentee using non-directive approaches such as the Socratic method. You learned that mentoring today employs **cross-gender** and **cross-cultural** mentoring to broaden mentees' horizons. Next, you learned that mentoring can be highly **structured** or **informal**; it can be **long term** or **short term**. Finally, you learned that mentoring is not just a job to a real mentor; that mentors truly **care beyond the work**.

Creating a Mentoring Relationship

Having someone to tell it to is one of the fundamental needs of human beings."

–Miles Franklin

In this part:

Stages of Development

As in any relationship of two or more people, mentoring can be described using Dr. Bruce Tuckman's Five Stages of Development model[1].

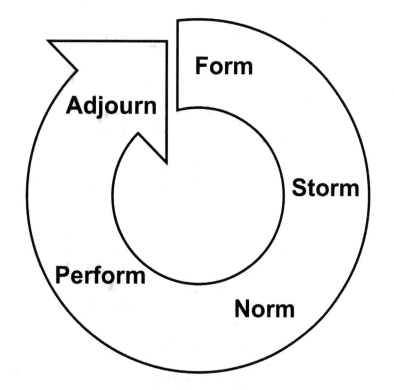

The first stage is **Form**, where people get to know one another and (hopefully) talk about their expectations for the relationship. The next stage is called **Storm.** This is where people learn what it is like to work together. Assumptions are tested and interpersonal dynamics become evident. The key here is to make sure that issues are dealt with directly and promptly. If they are not, then the issues become part of the next stage. **Norm** is the general way that we work together. It's the kind of "normalcy" or day-to-day experience of being or working together. When we have a norm where issues are addressed effectively, the relationship moves to the next stage. **Perform** is a high performance stage. Things tend to go well and when issues come up they are addressed. The last stage, **Adjourn,** is when the mentoring relationship ends. This stage should include honor for the work that was done and gratitude for the time invested. It is a time to say goodbye. This stage is very important but it is often overlooked.

If the Form stage is successful, many mentoring pitfalls can be avoided. The more effort spent on this state, the more successful the mentoring relationship is likely to be. This stage is the basis for future expectations and interactions.

---

[1] Tuckman, B.W., & Jensen, M.A. (1977). *Stages of small-group development revisited.* Group Org. Studies 2:419-217.

Where to Begin

OK, you have decided to become a mentor. Here is a quick list of things you might want to ask yourself to test your readiness.

► Do you know why you are doing this?

► Are you ready, willing, and able to mentor others? How do you know?

► Are you emotionally prepared to invest time and effort to help another person? What is the evidence that you are prepared?

► Do you have the time, skills, and freedom to devote yourself to another person? How much time do you actually have?

► How will this impact your work and your family time?

► Are you ready to make such a commitment? What is your track record of following through on commitments to others?

How did you do on this self-test? Take a moment to write down a few of your reactions to this list.

_____

_____

_____

As described in the last part, a mentoring relationship can be short term or long term. It can be formal or informal. What quadrant does the proposed mentoring relationship fall into? Making the commitment to mentor is a big step and a serious offering of your time and energy. Take some time to consider its potential impact on your life, such as the additional demands mentoring will place on your time.

Mentoring requires an awareness of the needs of others and a willingness to pause and listen for a while. Do you have these skills? Can you offer them easily? Mentoring will mean occasional inconveniences and less time for other priorities such as family commitments and personal activities.

Before you begin a mentoring relationship, be clear in your reasons for committing to it. Discuss with your potential mentee the reasons for beginning a mentoring relationship. The two of you should agree on these reasons before making any commitments.

Once you have tasted success as a mentor, you will probably want to mentor again.

The Mentoring Match

It is critical to match the mentor and mentee if the relationship is to succeed. Assess the mentor's resources and the mentee's needs rather than make assumptions. This will help to clarify expectations. The matrix below shows the relationship between the mentee's needs and the mentor's resources. Discuss needs vs. resources at the beginning of the relationship.

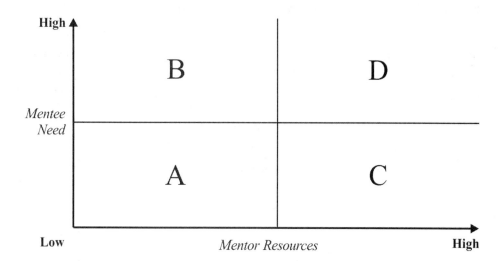

Quadrant A: The mentor's resources and mentee's needs are low, spontaneous, or occasional. Very short-term interventions may be adequate.

Quadrant B: The mentee's need is high and the mentor's resources, time, skills, etc., are low. Helping the mentee find a more appropriate mentor or professional help may be appropriate.

Quadrant C: The mentor's resources are substantial, but the mentee's needs are low. Occasional help may be all that is needed, and the mentor may have time and resources to help others.

Quadrant D: The mentee's need is high and the mentor's resources are abundant. The potential exists for a structured, effective and productive relationship.

The mentor and mentee should discuss their respective willingness, readiness, and personality. Aligning these elements can produce a good match. A very willing mentor trying to work with a mentee who perceives little need for help is inappropriate. In the same way, a needy mentee and an overloaded mentor may not work well together.

The mentor or the mentee might move to different quadrants during the mentoring relationship. Frequent status reviews are strongly recommended. Reviews serve as critical feedback for monitoring the relationship. These might be conducted on a weekly basis at first, then at longer intervals as the relationship progresses. Two-way communication is the life-blood of a mentoring relationship.

WHAT DO YOU BRING TO THE TABLE?

Mentors bring a variety of resources to a mentoring situation. They vary by job, personality, interests, experiences, friends, associates, available time, and energy. Identify some of the specific resources you could bring to the mentoring table. List as many items as you can think of. Use more paper if you need it.

My current work position:

_____

_____

My past work experiences:

_____

_____

My education, training, certifications, and so on:

_____

_____

Professional organizations with whom I am affiliated:

_____

_____

My pastimes, hobbies, and/or clubs:

_____

_____

Things I am passionate about:

_____

_____

Any other assets:

_____

_____

Sometimes it is helpful to ask someone who knows you well to give his/her perspective on these items. Often they have useful input.

Determining Mentee Expectations

You should define mentee expectations in the Form stage, which is the first step in the Stages of Development model.

Relationships can sometimes end in disappointment. This is usually caused by unmet expectations on one or both sides. Some of these expectations might not have been expressed at the start of the relationship. Expectations often spring from the subconscious and sometimes don't surface until a quarrel erupts.

The mentor and mentee must have a frank conversation about what each expects from the relationship. Failure to do this could cause serious problems in the mentoring relationship.

For example, some firms have downsized operations and laid off midlevel managers and professional workers. News stories have detailed the complaints of laid off employees claiming that their mentors failed to take care of them. "When the going got tough, he worried more about his own career than he did about mine," said one young professional.

It is unlikely that the mentor and mentee in this case ever discussed whose career came first. Yet the mentee had that expectation and complained when the mentor failed to meet it. This assumption would make sense only if both parties had agreed that the mentor would be responsible for the mentee's job security.

Understanding Mentee Expectations

Here are three ways to test both parties' understanding of the mentee's expectations:

▶ Ask the mentee to write a brief description of what he or she expects to gain from the relationship—short term and long term.

▶ Ask the mentee to briefly explain the roles and responsibilities of each party in the relationship.

▶ Ask the mentee to list any special needs or features of the relationship that should be considered in developing the relationship.

As the mentor learns the mentee's expectation, the mentor should reserve judgment and ask questions. The goal of this exercise is to derive an honest statement of expectations from the mentee. If the mentee's expectations are more than the mentor is willing to accept, they should be discussed until there is either alignment or until both parties acknowledge that this might not be a good match.

These conversations can be challenging and even uncomfortable, but issues that are not discussed at this stage in the relationship will simply emerge later. It may require much more effort to resolve them later. If the issues cannot be solved, they can derail the relationship.

The ideal mentoring relationship is one of honesty and open communication. The Form stage is the best point to build that into the relationship.

Acknowledging that each of us has needs and being open and honest about them can help make our expectations explicit. Failing to state our expectations of another person is natural but unfair. Mentees and mentors need to be explicit about what they hope to gain from the relationship. This helps both parties determine if the match is likely to be a good one.

The goal during the Forms stage is to get all expectations on the table as early as possible with patience and respect. In this way both the mentor and the mentee understand what the other person wants from the relationship.

"See these white highlights in my hair?
Well, that makes me the mentor."

EXPECTATIONS

Please answer these questions regarding the mentee's expectations. Use more paper if you need it.

1. How will you as the mentor meet each of the mentee's stated expectations?

_____

_____

_____

2. What are your reactions to the mentee's perception of the roles and responsibilities of each party in the relationship?

_____

_____

_____

3. What are your reactions to the special needs of the mentee?

_____

_____

_____

4. If a discussion about expectations highlighted any differences, can they be resolved? How will you and the mentee resolve these differences?

_____

_____

_____

At this point, both the mentor and the mentee should be able to discern how close or far apart they are regarding the match between them. Further dialogue could better align expectations. Do not proceed with the mentoring relationship until you have resolved these items.

Developing a Partnership

Our perceptions going into a mentoring relationship can shape how that relationship ends. For example, mentoring is sometimes perceived as a one-way street, with the mentor giving and the mentee receiving. This top-down, parent/child view of the relationship is often based on the assumption that the mentee:

▶ Is not able to do much for him/herself,

▶ Is not in a position to do much in return,

▶ Should be a dutiful and appreciative mentee,

▶ Doesn't bring much to the table, and

▶ Can't teach the mentor something through this experience.

The top-down approach is especially prevalent in organizations where the mentor is a senior person and the mentee is a junior. It can be difficult to engage in an adult conversation as peers. This reinforces the giver-receiver aspect of the relationship. In the past the senior/junior relationship seemed so natural that few people questioned the assumptions on which it was based.

This severely limited relationship often worked, resulting in career success for the mentee and a sense of parental satisfaction for the mentor. But this type of mentoring produces clones and today it prepares employees to succeed in a world that no longer exists. Today's global workforce of diverse, highly competent, and tech-savvy workers are unlikely to tolerate a condescending relationship. The workplace requires adult conversations if employees and their companies are to succeed.

Successful mentoring is a partnership in which the mentor and mentee freely contribute to the discussions. They work together as partners with mutual respect. A mentor might have more experience or insight, but the relationship can be one of sharing and true collaboration. Both parties should share a goal of personal and professional advancement.

One way to think of it is that the mentor helps but the mentee does. One without the other wouldn't be a very effective mentoring relationship.

Guiding Principles

The Glue

When couples marry, they exchange vows. Scouts recite an oath. American citizens say the Pledge of Allegiance. Followers of some faiths profess a creed.

In mentoring, the concept of guiding principles has the same effect when used with aligned intent. While the mentor and the mentee are still in the form stage, both need to define the characteristics of the relationship. Examples might include trust, confidentiality, constructive candor, trust intent, confronting issues immediately, responding to calls within 24 hours, avoiding texting, and so on.

What does each party want or need as guiding principles? List specific behaviors that you think will support and deepen the relationship. One possible principle is entered as an example.	
Mentor	**Mentee**
Open to change	Open to change

By creating this list, both parties agree to be held accountable for exercising these behaviors within the mentoring relationship.

ASSESSING PERSONAL EXPECTATIONS

As a mentor you should take two steps to reaffirm your commitment to this relationship. In the first step you assess your motivations and needs in this relationship. The second step is to share this information with your mentee.

Some mentors say that they don't expect anything, and sometimes it is even true. But that might simply meant these mentors are unaware of their expectations.

Please answer the following questions.

1. What are your personal expectations for this relationship?

   _____

   _____

2. What type(s) of recognition do you expect and from whom do you want it?

   _____

   _____

3. What rewards do you expect to receive?

   _____

   _____

4. What other expectations do you have?

   _____

   _____

5. Would you be willing to share these hopes or expectations with your mentee? If not, why not?

   _____

   _____

You cannot do a kindness too soon, for you never know how soon it will be too late."

–Ralph Waldo Emerson

Creating a Mentor/Mentee Agreement

As we discussed, part of the mentoring glue is a written agreement listing the criteria for the relationship. This agreement documents:

1. The expectations._____

2. Required behaviors._____

3. The frequency of meetings._____

4. How progress is measured. _____

5. How success is defined. _____

Depending on the type of mentoring relationship, this agreement will be more or less specific and structured. We strongly recommend that all of these items be addressed in the mentoring agreement. Doing so does not mean it has to be restrictive or overly structured. The table below shows some examples.

Expectations	Less Structured	More Structured
How often will we meet?	Once each week. The mentee will arrange it.	Every Thursday at 2:00 p.m.
How will we measure progress?	We will both give verbal feedback as necessary.	At the end of each month we will each prepare a bulleted list.

Both parties must be clear about how they will address expectations. Do not rely on separate memories. Each party should have a copy of the written expectations.

The goal of the agreement is to set objectives. This must be a living document, so that mentor and mentee can discuss and implement changes along the way.

Key Development Activities

Whether you have a written or verbal agreement, mentor and mentee need to check the progress of the agreement. To do this you can establish specific key development activities, or KDAs. Examples of KDAs include:

▶ We will review guiding principles weekly.

▶ Mentee will join Internet networking sites.

▶ Mentee will create a two-minute elevator speech to describe career goals.

KDAs are specific goals and activities that can be evaluated for completeness and quality. They should be checked periodically—weekly at first and then monthly. Mentor and mentee should discuss all of the KDAs that are relevant to the relationship. At these review sessions, the KDAs can be revised with mutual agreement.

KDAs: TESTING PROGRESS ALONG THE WAY

List some KDAs that a mentoring agreement might contain.

1. _____
2. _____
3. _____
4. _____
5. _____
6. _____

What are some issues that could arise from these KDAs?

1. _____
2. _____
3. _____
4. _____
5. _____
6. _____

Man is a knot into which relationships are tied..."

– Antoine de Saint-Exupéry

Two-Way Mentoring / Reverse Mentoring

Some of the best mentors assume that they and their mentees are in a lifelong process of personal development and that mentoring relationships go both ways. While the mentee realizes greater potential and development, the mentor also learns and grows.

Technology advances have made the concept of "reverse mentoring" a widely used tool. Jack Welch, former Chairman of General Electric, ordered his top 600 managers to reach down into the various levels of the organization and learn from (be mentored by) Internet junkies. Often that created a "younger teaching older" relationship, which runs counter to traditional mentoring. In reverse mentoring the mentor in the relationship is the less obvious person, such as the junior employee.

When contemplating the "generation match-up" of a mentoring relationship, consider some of the focus areas that the two of you could include and prioritize.

> ▶ Focus on basic principles, fundamental truths, and the assumptions associated with them.
>
>> This can be both enlightening and frightening. While both people might learn something, it can be unsettling to challenge assumptions about truisms or belief in fundamental truths. People like certainty. When beliefs are challenged the believer can get anxious and even defensive. To succeed one must be open to reassessment and discussion.
>
> ▶ Stay current with new developments and their implications.
>
>> This focus area addresses new technologies, research, industry changes, and innovations. This can be a valuable knowledge- and skill-building exercise.
>
> ▶ Grow interpersonal skills.
>
>> Sometimes the most valuable lessons are in interpersonal competence. Getting along with others is critical for work and personal life. Skills like active listening, effective communication, and conflict management are critical skills. Without them, success in any part of life quite often is severely limited.

Effective mentoring can have profound impact in each of these areas. Can you think of others?

TWO WAY MENTORING

What does two-way mentoring mean to you in your role as mentor or mentee? Answer the questions below; then share the answer with your mentoring partner to serve as the basis for a dialogue.

Do you think the mentor has assumptions about learning from this relationship? What are those assumptions?

_____

_____

What could the mentor learn from this relationship in addition to the stated goals of the mentee?

_____

_____

Reverse Mentoring

In a reverse mentoring relationship, what might get in the way of a younger mentor working with an older mentee?

_____

_____

How can each participant in the relationship deal with these challenges?

_____

_____

From your perspective, what are some of the specific benefits of reverse mentoring?

_____

_____

CASE STUDY: Gen and Manuel

Gen is an intelligent 22-year-old who just joined the company as a highly skilled IT manager specializing in network engineering and information assurance. After work she keeps in touch with her friends via Twitter and Facebook. While in college she created online study groups for high school students in several countries. The study groups hold virtual meetings using standard web conferencing software that they download free of charge from the Internet. The goal of the study groups is to help students in other countries learn about technology so that they can expand their career choices.

Gen's native culture discourages outspokenness. This is even more true for women than for men. Despite her education, the time she has spent in the United States, and her experience in the tech field, Gen still feels influenced by her native culture's customs. There are times when she refrains from speaking up, and this is particularly true when interacting with men.

Manuel's proud family can trace its roots back to their arrival in the Americas nearly 400 years ago. His specialty is operations research, and his role in the company is to help the Chicago regional vice president create process improvements, and to advise on production strategy. Gen is Manuel's peer and they have the same boss.

While the company has done well since its founding 20 years ago, revenue is starting to fall off. Baby boomers still represent the bulk of the company's core customers.

Manuel has met Gen once. Even though he is 20 years older, Manuel is intrigued by how much she knows.

1. What career opportunities might exist in this scenario?

_____

_____

2. If Manuel decided to pursue these opportunities, how might he go about it?

_____

_____

CONTINUED

3. What are some possible challenges or issues?

_____

_____

4. Who within the company might be able to help Manuel pursue these opportunities?

_____

_____

How would your responses differ if Gen was a male?

How might your responses differ if you had been raised in Gen's culture? In Manuel's?

Compare your responses to those of the author in the Appendix.

Part Summary

In this part, you learned Tuckman's **stages of development** in a relationship. Next, you learned **how to begin** a mentoring relationship. You learned the importance of the **mentoring match**, and of identifying mentee **expectations**. Then you learned how to **develop** a partnership, and to set **guiding principles**. You learned how to create a mentor/mentee **agreement**. Finally, you learned about **two-way** mentoring and **reverse** mentoring.

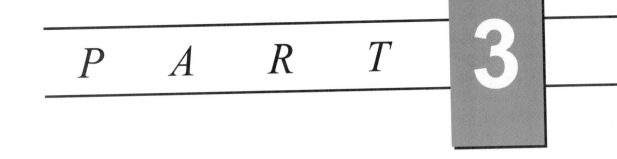

PART 3

Maintaining a

Mentoring

Relationship

Success is to be measured not so much by the position that one has reached in life as by the obstacles which he has overcome."

–Booker T. Washington

In this part:

- ▶ Adopting a Change Attitude
- ▶ Managing Change
- ▶ Coping Mechanics
- ▶ Mirroring
- ▶ Validation
- ▶ It's Rarely Black or White
- ▶ Progressive Adaptation

Adopting a Change Attitude

Let's face it—the main reason to engage in a mentoring relationship is a hope for change. That change could be in terms of thinking differently and/or behaving differently. Otherwise, why would one willingly participate in a mentoring relationship? So let's assume the mentee or protégé recognizes that a mentoring relationship will have an impact. This means that some kind of change will (hopefully) occur as a result of the mentoring experience.

Some people are resistant to change, but the author feels that human beings are well-designed for change. We have the built-in capacity to adapt to change. However, when we are confused about change, that is when we quite often become resistant to it. The mentor and mentee should be on the lookout for resistance to change. If it is observed, then both parties should dialogue about the resistance and the reasons for it.

Mark Twain once said, "I have experienced many problems in my lifetime, most of which never happened." This humorous observation can apply to a mentoring relationship. Fears can prevent either party from moving toward something new. Often these fears are groundless.

By its nature the mentoring process calls upon the mentee to consider changes. The changes might be generated by a challenging opportunity, a personal insight, or something that is forced upon the mentee. In mentoring, change is the name of the game, whether it is self-imposed, optional, or imposed from without.

Both parties should maintain an open mind that welcomes change. There may be a sense of loss from giving up familiar and comfortable beliefs, behaviors, or relationships. There may be fear of the unknown or of possible failure. The best prescription for dealing with these issues is frequent, candid, constructive, caring dialogue.

READING RESISTANCE

Mentees can display resistance to change in a number of ways. They might be overtly resistant by saying one of the following:

"Well, I'm not going to try that because I like how I do it now."

"That's not an area I want to discuss."

"I won't consider that."

Consider the kind of "resistance to change" comments that could come up during a mentoring relationship and list a few below.

1. _____

2. _____

3. _____

Resistance can also be expressed non-verbally through facial expressions, tone of voice, gestures, or posture. List three non-verbal ways a mentee might signal resistance in a non-verbal manner.

1. _____

2. _____

3. _____

What kinds of issues might be behind resistance to change?

1. _____

2. _____

3. _____

Managing Change

When a mentee experiences significant change, several things are necessary to adapt successfully. To deal with change, the mentee must:

▶ Understand the reason for the change.

▶ Have a clear understanding of what the situation will be after the change.

▶ Have time to absorb the new understanding. This should take place on the mentee's schedule, not the mentor's. But the mentor must be on the lookout for resistance or procrastination, and address those if necessary.

▶ Define any new behaviors and allow time to adjust and modify those behaviors.

▶ Discuss possible coping mechanisms to manage the stress that can come with change.

▶ Set aside a time to reflect on the process and on the meaning of the change. These reflections should be shared with the mentor.

Context shifting is key to this process. Context shifting occurs when a person adjusts thoughts, perspectives, or belief about something. When this happens, the context in which the person relates to that something shifts. People are more likely to make changes that move them toward a goal if they can clearly imagine what their world will be like after the change. The context shift should be imagined in positive terms. For example, how will a situation or behavior improve? The mentor must help the mentee to shift his or her mental context from the current reality to the one that points the way to what could be.

This will take time. Instant change is rare. We have found that slow change gives the mentee time to acclimate.

It can be helpful to include patience as one of the guiding principles, and to give periodic feedback on the relationship's patience.

Coping Mechanisms

To cope is to deal with and overcome difficulties. Coping mechanisms can be used to deal with the stress that might come from change.

Here are some things to consider when coping with the stress that might arise from the changes brought on by mentoring.

▶ Recognize the stress. Sometimes just naming the feeling can help.

▶ Understand the source of the stress. The mentor can help the mentee by discussing the sources or causes of stress.

▶ Get additional support. This might include family members, friends, and co-workers. Avoid negative people when you are undergoing stress.

▶ Get away. Take time off—an evening, an hour, an afternoon, a whole day, or a week. Get the space you need to reflect on what's happening.

▶ Set limits. Everyone wants to be liked, and this can make it hard to say no. But learn to set appropriate boundaries.

▶ Choose what's important. You don't need to be involved in everything that goes on at work or at home. Save your energy for the things that really matter, and that really need your input.

▶ Create healthy outlets. Read, play sports, exercise, volunteer, get a hobby, or do any combination of these. All work and no play….

▶ Get help. If you need a professional to counsel you through the hardest times, don't be too egotistical to seek help. You wouldn't hesitate to go to an expert if your car's electronic fuel injection needed work. The human brain is even more complicated than that.

RESISTANCE AND STRESS BUSTERS

Think of the many changes and stressors that have been part of your life in the past. List a few of them on the lines below.

_____

_____

What were some things that you did (coping mechanisms) to deal with these changes and stressors that you listed above. It would be important to give this some thorough thought and be as specific as possible. Be sure to list the things that you did that might not have been positive. Include both in your list.

_____

_____

_____

Of the coping mechanisms that you listed above, which ones might be able to be used in a mentoring relationship to help manage and maintain a healthy mentoring relationship?

_____

_____

_____

How will you build these Resistance and Stress Busters into your mentoring relationship?

_____

_____

_____

Some have been thought brave because they were afraid to run away."

–Thomas Fuller

Mirroring

Mirroring is a psychological term that describes a relationship dynamic between two people. Mirroring shapes our sense of who we are. Our sense of self can change over time through personal growth and it is influenced by those around us. For example, we may feel confident at home or around peers and colleagues, but tentative or unassertive around authority figures.

Mirroring includes feedback, where people validate or confirm aspects of who they see themselves as. Validation builds confidence. Once something is mirrored back to us, we believe in it more strongly. Authority figures usually have a greater influence when it comes to mirroring. Our parents or our bosses strongly influence our overall sense of "what it means to be me." Mentors ideally play a very strong role when it comes to mirroring. We know who we are in two ways. They are:

▶ How we view ourselves.

▶ How others view us.

If our internal sense doesn't match what is reflected back from the rest of the world, we have two choices. One is to consider it as truth and grow from it. The other is to deny it and continue with current behaviors. What we do with that feedback makes all the difference in a mentoring relationship. Some examples of mirroring are:

▶ "I'm not sure you're aware of this, but I've noticed that whenever Mary speaks up in a meeting you cut her off or dismiss her idea, before she has a chance to explain her position."

▶ "I know it took courage to speak up in that meeting and I want you to know that I really appreciated your honesty."

▶ "You seem to have a lot of explanations for why this project isn't working, and most are complaints about others. Is it possible that we should look at your part in this?"

Questions that can be asked in an effort to use mirroring in a coaching or mentoring relationship might include:

▶ How would you define who you are as a person or as a professional?

▶ How do you know the answer to the question above?

▶ What sources do you use for this definition?

▶ Are the sources reliable? How do you know?

▶ Are there other sources of mirroring that could be used for a reality check?

▶ What fears do you have about hearing from other mirrors?

▶ How can you use what you learn about yourself in this mentoring relationship in your personal life?

All of us need confidence and a positive self-image. The way in which individuals respond to problems reflects that their feelings about themselves or their general perception of self. Research indicates that two-thirds of the population suffers from low self-esteem. They have negative feelings about themselves or about attributes they possess.

Focusing on deficiencies can make it difficult to be motivated or to make positive changes. A mentor's primary role is to provide genuine confidence-building insights and experiences.

A less-appreciated means of damaging one's self-image can be the way the mentee talks to or about him/herself. Virtually everyone carries on an inner monologue. This inner conversation can be negative if it focuses on failure or shortcomings. Many of us, in fact, have been taught to deprecate our achievements rather than revel in them. This pulls down our spirits and sense of achievement. Is it any surprise that so many have trouble taking advantage of inherent talents? It is one thing to suffer a defeat and feel discouraged but quite another to beat yourself up over it.

A mentor can:

▶ Listen to discouragement issue without being judgmental.

▶ Provide an opportunity to vent or express negative feelings.

▶ Suggest remedies.

▶ Offer mirroring as a means to help.

Can you think of other things a mentor could do?

"Frankly, I was hoping you would be MY mentor."

Validation

Validation means proving something to be valid, or confirming or verifying its validity. Validation is important in a mentoring relationship.

When a mentor tells a mentee that their feelings are understandable in a given situation, the mentee benefits. This is a form of empathizing without saying they are right or wrong—no judgment. Encouraging a mentee to talk things through, especially negative issues, can help the mentee to move beyond them. Listening and empathizing without agreeing or disagreeing is validation, and it is an important mentoring technique. Some validating comments might include:

▶ Jim, if I had been in your shoes I would have felt the same way.

▶ Sally, a long time ago I was faced with a similar situation and at the time I did the exact same thing because I thought that was best.

▶ Peter and Nancy lead the team on this project. Their insight and intuition enabled us to complete the task in the most effective manner possible.

Notice that in some of the preceding examples, the speaker did not say that anything was right or wrong. They simply acknowledged what was. A mentor must remain neutral and non-judgmental to use this technique successfully.

MIRRORING AND VALIDATING WITHOUT AGREEING

List at least three specific responses you might make that would be a form of mirroring.

1. _____
2. _____
3. _____

For you, what might be some challenging elements of being able to use this skill effectively?

_____

_____

_____

List at least three specific responses you might make that would be a form of validation.

1. _____
2. _____
3. _____

For you, what might be some challenging elements of being able to use this skill effectively?

_____

_____

_____

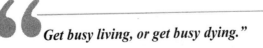

Get busy living, or get busy dying."

–Stephen King

It's Rarely Black or White

Dealing with the grey areas is important in a healthy mentoring relationship. Helping someone to grow as a person or as a professional is not always straightforward or simple. If we lived in a black-and-white world in which everything could be expressed as either/or, then mentoring could be reduced to a simple checklist. But real life isn't that simple.

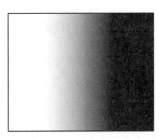

Mentees have their own lives, with a variety of demands from a variety of sources, and those demands change daily. Every day we each change, evolve, grow older, meet new people, encounter new problems and challenges, and perhaps suffer some defeats. No matter how little we seem to change, remaining the same is impossible. This applies to the mentor, too. The nature of the mentoring relationship is fluid and ever-evolving. This is why we need to understand grey areas.

Black and white thinking is occasionally appropriate. For example, most of us believe that there is no grey area when it comes to stealing, murder, smashing someone's car and driving away, or knowingly telling a lie. All of us know the difference between right and wrong, good and bad, helpful and not helpful. These are probably good times to think and act in "black and white."

There are times in a mentoring relationship when a black and white approach is not helpful. When confronting a black and white situation, consider the following:

▶ Watch for words like: never, always, can't, won't shouldn't, should. Listen for the use of absolutes such as: "I *never* seem to get along with my bosses," or "He gets to me *every* time we have a conversation." Stated absolutes seem accurate to the speaker, but may or may not be valid.

▶ Be careful of leaps of abstraction—jumping from observation to assumption and (over)generalization.

▶ Don't insist that your ideas represent the only reality.

▶ Learn to accept ambiguity.

▶ Don't jump to conclusions.

▶ Don't generalize based on a single example.

▶ Be curious.

▶ Update your beliefs when your perspective is broadened.

Acknowledging and discussing black and white can be a good starting point for addressing a problem.

Remember, life—and mentoring—is rarely black and white.

Progressive Adaptation

Progressive adaptation is the process of accepting new ways of thinking and doing. A weight-loss program is a physical progressive adaptation. A person on a weight loss program transforms before our eyes over time. If it is a large amount of weight, the progression can be dramatic. Practicing a skill or sport is another example. Slowly but surely there is evidence that the person is changing and doing things differently.

A mentee goes through progressive adaptation during the mentoring relationship. Some mentee adaptations might not be dramatic or immediately noticeable. They tend to be gradual and unless the mentor is looking for them, they can go unnoticed. Sometimes the changes might not occur until after the mentoring relationship is over and the mentee has had time to fully reflect on the mentoring experience.

Use the following tips to gauge how the mentoring partners are adapting:

> ▶ Pick up on subtle concerns the other person articulates, such as, "Well it really doesn't matter," or a brusque "I'm fine."

> ▶ Observe small or gradual changes that seem significant, such as changes in appearance, dress, or punctuality.

> ▶ Look for verbal signals, such as tone of voice or negativity seeping in to the conversation.

> ▶ Read non-verbal signals, such as avoiding eye contact, continuously turning away, or sitting with crossed arms and legs.

These signs aren't red flags. Just be on the lookout for signals that might indicate a reason for concern. These signals can be clues that something is a little off and the help might be needed.

Be observant. Don't jump to conclusions. Ask question and watch for inconsistent behavior. When adaptation occurs, ask yourself if it adheres to the guiding principles that both parties agreed to.

SETTING MUTUAL PARAMETERS

Dealing effectively with small problems to keep them from becoming large ones is a shared responsibility. However, the mentor should take the lead to keep the relationship on track.

Identify at least three verbal or non-verbal clues that suggest a mentee is having problems on the job:

1. _____
2. _____
3. _____

Identify at least three patterns of behavior that might indicate the mentee is experiencing difficulty in his or her personal life:

1. _____
2. _____
3. _____

Identify at least three repetitive complaints from a mentee that might indicate an unresolved or possibly emerging personal difficulty:

1. _____
2. _____
3. _____

> *Reach high, for stars lie hidden in your soul.*
> *Dream deep, for every dream precedes the goal."*
>
> **–Pamela Vaull Starr**

CASE STUDY: Paula

Paula is a very bright and sparkling person you met in the company cafeteria. She works for Harold Greening in Accounts Payable.

You served as an informal mentor to Paula on three or four occasions in the last few weeks when she wanted to talk about a problem she has with her finances. You listened, were nondirective in your responses, and gave her information when she asked for it. She said you were very helpful. She also solved her financial problem in a clever way that never occurred to you.

You learned that Paula graduated from high school and has a certificate in secretarial sciences from a local business school. She seems well-trained, but not well-educated. Her perspective on the world is limited, as is her experience. Yet she seems fascinated with the variety and challenges you encounter in your job. Her understanding of the difference between your work and lifestyle and hers has led her to talk about changing her life to one that is more challenging and diverse.

You have heard that she is a hard worker and quick to catch on. You believe she is capable of great things, but she seems unaware of her natural intelligence and abilities. This comes out in her conversation when she discounts compliments about her intelligence and ability.

You believe that if her self-image and self-confidence were to rise, she would be more willing to acknowledge and express her strengths.

1. If you decide to continue informally mentoring Paula, what special aspects of mentoring would you emphasize?

_____

_____

_____

2. Would your mentoring be affected if you were a male? How?

_____

_____

_____

CONTINUED

3. How would you attempt to make Paula more aware of her special abilities and talents?

_____

_____

_____

4. How would you convey to her the importance of speaking positively about herself?

_____

_____

_____

5 In what specific ways could you help Paula?

_____

_____

_____

Compare your responses with those of the author in the Appendix.

Part Summary

In this part, you learned how to adopt a **change attitude** to help adapt to the changes brought about by mentoring. You learned that change is a natural part of the mentoring process, but that you must manage change through processes such as **context shifting**. Next, you learned **coping mechanisms** to help you deal with the stress that can sometimes come from change. You learned to use **mirroring** to help you see yourself. Then, you learned to use **validation** to express support while remaining neutral and non-judgmental. You learned that mentoring deals with **grey** areas and that things are rarely black and white. Finally, you learned that many mentees experience **progressive adaptation** as a way to incorporate change.

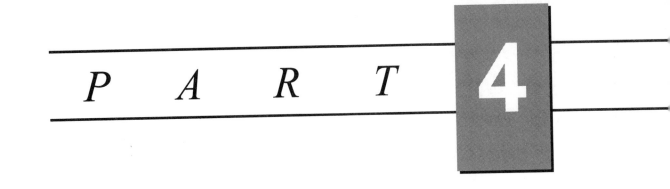

Navigating the Mentoring Relationship

"A lot of people have gone further than they thought they could because someone else thought they could."

–Zig Ziglar

In this part:

▶ Effective Mentoring Tools

▶ Shifting Context

▶ Active Listening

▶ Naming Feelings

▶ Listening for Motivation

▶ Constructive Confrontation

▶ Information That Has Positive Impact

▶ Giving Permission

▶ Being Genuinely Curious

Effective Mentoring Tools

We have discussed how to define, create, and maintain a mentoring relationship. This part will focus on how to navigate the mentoring relationship by using specific relational and dialogical tools.

The mentoring relationship has many facets. Below are several tools that can be particularly helpful to the mentee's development during this relationship.

1. **Shifting context.** Help a mentee envision a positive future or outcome. Encourage a different way to think about his or her situation.

2. **Listening actively.** Be a listener with whom the mentee can, without judgment, bounce thoughts and ideas around.

3. **Naming feelings.** Actively engage in talking about the mentee's feelings. Feeling can be helpful motivators for the mentee to make changes.

4. **Enabling constructive confrontation.** Confront issues in ways that deepen the relationship and do not cause damage.

5. **Providing information that has positive impact.** Bring knowledge and understanding to the relationship. Share ideas, suggest possible solutions, and offer advice.

6. **Giving permission.** Allow the mentee to be who s/he is without judgment. This has the effect of empowerment. This boosts the mentee's self-confidence and can help counteract any negative elements.

7. **Being genuinely curious.** Help the mentee consider possibilities beyond the obvious. Genuine curiosity has the effect of providing new and enriching experiences, often when you least expect them.

These tools can encourage a mentee's personal growth and solidify the mentoring relationship. The tools don't meet all of the mentee's needs, but they can have a profound impact when used at just the right moment.

Shifting Context

Imagination plays a role in the vision of successful people. It can be a pivotal component of personal development. We have all heard the expression, "if you can imagine it, you can be it." A mentee might need help imagining alternatives to current situations. The mentee's ability to imagine something different for his/her life is an important component for success. A gloomy outlook on the future can precede failure or lack of change.

Mentors can bring imagination to the relationship. A shift in mentee context might already exist—imagining a clearer, healthier, or more successful future. If that shift does not exist, the mentor must help the mentee explore different ways of thinking about the future. A clear vision of the future will help a mentee realize that future.

A context shift often occurs at a subconscious level. For example, employees who receive promotions may begin to behave in ways that match their new perceptions of themselves. Creating a personal concept of what success would look like can motivate a person to make real and sustained change. Successful people use this mental stimulus to guide them to where they want to be.

However, even the best of us can get stuck. Sometimes we rely on outmoded visions and habits that don't serve us well. Some might say, "Because I never finished college, I will never be promoted." Without a context shift, one might wallow in despair. A vision of achieving success—a context shift—can inspire each of us.

Mentors play a critical roll in helping the mentee to envision desired goals and to move toward their fulfillment.

CASE STUDY: Carly

Carly Ditton worked for 10 years as a bookkeeper for a large retail chain. Early in her career she was rated as an employee with great potential. She was mentored during her career and received several promotions. She and her husband put off having children so that she could focus on her career. Despite her success, she lost interest in her work and began to feel restless.

One day while driving home from work she noticed a real estate sign in front of a home that she and her husband had admired. She began to imagine selling homes to people like herself. Each day that she drove past the sign, she became more excited by the vision of becoming a realtor, and began to wonder if this might be possible.

She made a list of conditions that would be necessary for her to succeed as a realtor. She felt this would be a good exercise to see if this was pure fantasy or if there was a possibility that she might become a realtor. She knew she already had many necessary attributes: she worked well with people, was articulate, organized, intelligent, and persistent.

Carly frequently revisited this list to imagine herself as a successful realtor. She shared the vision with her husband, who supported her desire to change careers. They both imagined that by using her realty contacts and knowledge they would be able to purchase a new home. They imagined starting a family.

Carly began taking classes to get her real estate license. Five years later she had built a career as a realtor. While she wasn't a millionaire, she was a success and she enjoyed her work. She and her husband had purchased a beautiful home and they were expecting their first child.

Carly believed the secret to her success was envisioning herself in this new role. She worked at vividly seeing, hearing, and feeling herself working as a realtor. She could smell flowers in the garden and could see children playing in the lush green yard of the home she imagined buying with her husband.

On the next page, envision one personal goal you would like to achieve—something that is actually possible, rather than, say, becoming a rock star despite having no musical training. Picture yourself being there. Focus on the what, not the how. Describe what it will be like when you achieve it.

Now, consider using this same type of envisioning exercise with your mentee to help him or her shift context to a positive future focus.

CONTINUED

Shifting through Visioning

Envision one personal goal you would like to achieve. Picture yourself being in a place where you have achieved that goal. Focus on the what, not the how. Describe what it will be like when you achieve it.

_____

_____

_____

_____

_____

_____

_____

Active Listening

Active listening helps sustain a healthy mentoring relationship. Active listening means that when you are conversing with another person, you are fully engaged. What does fully engaged mean? It means you:

- ▶ Make good eye contact.

- ▶ Respect the gift of dialogue that you are being offered.

- ▶ Don't become distracted by surroundings.

- ▶ Silence your cell phone.

- ▶ Maintain genuine, *real* curiosity.

- ▶ Nod from time to time to show involvement.

- ▶ Verbalize prompts, such as, "Really?," "Interesting," and "I can't believe it."

- ▶ Restate points to make sure you understood them correctly.

We have all wished for someone to talk to when things bother us. Getting something out in the open by talking about it with someone else offers a very therapeutic relief.

Mentees benefit from this experience. Active listening is probably the most powerful tool a mentor can offer. Active listening means providing an ear without taking on the other person's problems, giving advice, or joining them in the "ain't it awful" game. It is listening by truly hearing what is being said without judgment. The listener doesn't have to do anything but be there and be focused.

Active listening is the ability to become absorbed in what another person is saying, treating that person's words as confidential communication—almost like a gift— without injecting your own opinions. This gives the other person an opportunity to gain insight by articulating and sorting things out. The speaker might develop a solution, and almost always gains emotional release and relief. The other byproduct of this process is a deepening of the relationship.

Active listening means allowing a mentee to talk without interruption and accepting that what is being said is genuine, at least to the speaker. Listening to another person for that person's sake is not a discussion. You also listen during a discussion, but during active listening your role is to help another person sort out their thoughts and ideas.

Naming Feelings

When we name something, we gain power over it.

If I am upset over something but I am not quite sure what is bothering me, that something tends to control my emotions. Once I name it—pinpoint what it is—I can do something about it. This is gaining or regaining control.

When a mentee is speaking, the mentor should listen to the words said, but also listen for the underlying feelings. Feelings can be strong motivators. Facts are the objective reality, but how a person feels about those facts determines whether or not an issue exists. The person's feelings define the dimension of the problem and its level of importance.

For instance, "What time is it?" asked in a matter-of-fact voice reflects a need for information. The same question phrased as "Oh, no, what time is it?" and asked with urgency is quite a different message—it indicates a potential problem. The objective reality (the time of day) may be the same in both cases, but the expressed urgency in the second question implies a need for action.

Too great an emphasis on facts can make it hard to recognize the feelings of the people involved. Feelings are important because they motivate our actions—and an inability to detect feelings can cause us to miss the most important part of the message someone is sending.

Listening for Motivation

Researchers who study motivation state that there are four basic emotions: fear, anger, grief, and joy. These can range in intensity. Fear may range from a vague uneasiness to panic; anger may be minor annoyance or uncontrolled rage. Responses to emotions also vary. Fear or grief can be so repressed that there is no response until the emotion becomes overwhelming.

Emotions are often combined with thoughts. This leads to feelings such as disappointment, embarrassment, or satisfaction.

The capacity to detect the emotions and feelings and to respond appropriately is a critical art of mentoring. Because feelings can often motivate people, overlooking them can limit a mentor's effectiveness.

"I missed out on the recorder and went straight to the tuba.
I mean, where was the guidance?"

What's the Motivation?

Below are several statements a mentee might make. Identify the feelings and the possible motivations they might induce.

1. "It seems like a good idea… but I just don't know…"

   Feeling Expressed: *Ambivalence; finds the idea attractive but is afraid*

   Motivation: *To delay or avoid*

   Likely Action: *Little, late, or none*

2. "I just heard our company filed for bankruptcy!"

   Feeling Expressed: _____

   Motivation: _____

   Likely Action: _____

3. "Can you believe it? My supervisor just chewed me out in front of my co-workers!"

   Feeling Expressed: _____

   Motivation: _____

   Likely Action: _____

4. "This assignment could really open doors for me."

   Feeling Expressed: _____

   Motivation: _____

   Likely Action: _____

5. "I don't think I'll make it in this program—I'm too far behind."

   Feeling Expressed: _____

   Motivation: _____

   Likely Action: _____

LISTENING FOR FEELINGS

Below are three statements that might be made by a mentee. Once you have read each statement, please write your thoughts on what you think the underlying emotional message could be.

1. "When I first joined the organization, I really thought I was going to get somewhere. It's been two years now and I'm still doing the same old thing."

_____

_____

_____

2. "This is the type of work I can really sink my teeth into. I get so wrapped up in it I forget to go home. Sometimes I lie awake nights thinking about it."

_____

_____

_____

3. "When I made that presentation on Tuesday, I thought you'd support my position. Instead, you just sat there. You didn't open your mouth once. What's a mentor for anyway?"

_____

_____

_____

What are some mentor responses that could further the dialogue to better understand the feelings involved?

_____

_____

_____

_____

Constructive Confrontation

When creating the guiding principles for a mentoring relationship, many mentors and mentees include a statement like this one:

"We agree to confront issues immediately instead of avoiding them. We agree to be mutually respectful when we discuss difficult issues."

You can count on needing to confront something during a mentoring relationship. It comes with the commitment that you make to each other.

Sometimes the issue might be attitude, behavior, or decisions. We know that criticizing, threatening, or pressuring are usually not effective confrontational tools. They are not healthy for the relationship.

This is why constructive confrontation is a critical tool. Consider these steps when dealing with difficult issues.

Seven Steps for Constructive Confrontation

1. **Experience the conflict**. What did I just experience? Just try to feel the experience. Identify what the experience is like for you at that moment. Try not to do anything or decide on action at this point. Just experience it and identify what has just occurred.

2. **Decide to confront**. What does the experience mean? Is it important to the relationship? What might the other person have been thinking? Why did s/he act that way? Do I need to confront this or can I honestly let it go? The key word here is "honestly." If I am going to confront, what is my goal and which conflict mode represents the best chance of reaching that goal?

3. **Invite**. Creating the context for dealing with conflict is often hard and awkward. Meet in a neutral place, and then ask for help in understanding something that is confusing to you. Even if you think you are really clear about what happened, sometimes asking for clarity is heard in a way that makes it easier for the other person to discuss.

4. **Ask what's really going on.** This is usually the most challenging part of the process. Focus on real causes and not symptoms. Continue to peel back the layers of what happened until you find the root cause.

5. **Decide what each will do**. This is the most creative step in the process. This is where you can ask the collaborative question, "What doesn't exist that needs to exist so that we can both get what we need?"

6. **Summarize**. Write down what each of you are agreeing to and have committed to doing. Do not trust each others' recollection of what was said and agreed to. Over time, the specifics can get fuzzy. Agree to meet and discuss this issue again at a specific date and time.

7. **Follow Up**. This is where most conflict management breaks down. Both parties must follow up by discussing the issue. Ask "How are you feeling?" or "Did we get beyond the problem?" or "Is there anything else we need to do or say about the issue we discussed?" Failure to follow up can cause the problem to return.

Five Options for Dealing with Conflict

Competition is when one person is determined to win. This can often result in trying to force the other person to comply.

Collaboration is when you work together to answer the question, "What doesn't exist that needs to exist to get what we both need?" This option can be hard to achieve but tends to be the most sustainable.

Compromise is when both give up something to find a needed middle ground. This can be unsustainable if one or both gave up something they really wanted.

Avoidance is when one or both decide to not deal with the conflict. Sometimes this is a good temporary step if there is anger or hurt involved. It could be used as a kind of "time out."

Accommodation is when one person's needs are met at the expense of the other's. This is not always bad. Sometimes it is a true expression of giving or self-sacrifice.

If conflict cannot be resolved, the next best thing is to try to manage it as well as possible.

CASE STUDY: Ray

You are Chris Rodriguez, a highly successful account executive. You consistently generate the highest earnings for your division. Three months ago you were asked to participate in a formal mentoring program for new hires. You were assigned to mentor Ray Peterson during his first six months on the job.

Ray strikes you as hell-bent on getting to the top as soon as possible. You find nothing wrong with his ambition—it resembles your own. But you question some of his methods. Ray seems to devote most of his time and energy to making connections rather than demonstrating his abilities through performance.

Ray refers to work assignments from his supervisor as "busy work." He turns in "hastily performed, somewhat sloppy work," to quote his supervisor.

Your company downsized three years ago and eliminated several layers of management. The organization is now lean and mean with everyone carrying a heavy load. When you explained this to Ray, he saw an opportunity. "Fewer people to get in my way," he responded. He continued to behave as before.

Ray played up to you at first, but then interpreted your efforts to help him as "getting on my case." It would be easy to not recommend Ray for retention— and to warn him of your intention. But as his appointed mentor, you feel you should make a greater effort to salvage him. You are now at a place where you need to change how you deal with Ray.

CONTINUED

Dealing with Ray

1. What kinds of questions could you ask to better understand Ray's perceptions of corporate life? How might doing so be helpful?

_____

_____

_____

2. What specific behaviors might Ray be showing that indicate his perceptions of corporate life?

_____

_____

_____

3. Based on the concepts and tools discussed so far, what approach do you think would be most effective in dealing with Ray?

_____

_____

_____

4. Based upon your own experiences at work, what roles do internal competition and internal cooperation play in today's global, cross-cultural, professional, and highly technical society?

_____

_____

_____

Compare your responses with those of the author in the Appendix.

Information That Has Positive Impact

As we've seen, it's important that mentees take the initiative to instigate change in their lives. A mentor has many roles. One of those roles includes actively listening and sometimes confronting the mentee who makes an inappropriate decision or behaves inappropriately. Of course, the mentor explains so the mentee can understand, and occasionally provides information that the mentee can use in making decisions. The key for the mentor is to guide, not instruct.

When information is user-friendly (non-judgmental) and factual the mentee can store it away for future use. Since the mentor is typically not the mentee's supervisor, the mentor can only offer help, not force it on the mentee.

When a person with a problem is ready to resolve it, a mentor can provide relevant information, while still leaving responsibility for solving the problem to its owner. Sometimes a mentor can point the way to useful information, letting the mentee do his or her own research.

One or both of the parties should follow up these kinds of conversations. An easy way to do this is to remind the other party of the conversation and ask what their thoughts are now. This can be a terrific opportunity to revisit the issue in a reflective and relatively safe way.

Giving Permission

The role that giving permission plays in a mentoring relationship is an interesting one. Giving permission opens up a new space for the mentee to enter.

A mentee might have a fear of enjoying work, achieving recognition, or earning too much money. Sometimes these deep-seated psychological fears are beyond the scope of a mentoring relationship. But occasionally a mentor recognizes something in a mentee's past that seems to be an obstacle to success. In a situation such as this, giving permission can be helpful. Some examples include:

Mentee says...	Mentor gives permission...
All my life my parents told me not to take chances. They said to go for the sure thing.	I'm sure your parents have good reasons for giving you this advice. Let's take a small risk in this situation. I'll be here no matter what happens.
I've never been able to do that —never. I just don't think I can.	You know what? I think you can do it and I am giving you permission right here and now to try. What's the worst thing that can happen?

Permission acts like a counterweight to earlier inhibiting messages, constraints, or beliefs. We all have things in our past that impede our ability to resolve internal issues. A mentor should let a mentee know that it's okay overcome that past and take chances. Within certain limits, the mentee must also feel free to fail. We learn more from our failures than we do from our successes. An employee who is afraid to fail is also afraid to take risks.

This may sound simplistic, but to let go of our old thoughts of how we "should" be is very difficult. Mentors are uniquely poised to make a positive contribution to this dynamic.

Giving permission is a valuable gift from a mentor. When a mentor carefully and actively listens to the mentee, quite often the need for "giving permission" will become evident.

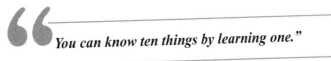

You can know ten things by learning one."

–Japanese Proverb

Being Genuinely Curious

When we are genuinely curious, we are better able to allow new opportunities and new learning into our life. It is when we consciously or unconsciously think that we "know all there is to know" about a given topic that we can short circuit new information as it comes in.

Some examples of "knowing it all" might include:

1. "I've been doing this job a long time. I know what I'm doing."

2. "I have a master's degree in finance so you don't need to tell me how to read a profit and loss statement."

3. "Look, I read that book and there is no way that the author was thinking that way."

In each of these statements and statements like them, there is an element of "there is nothing more I can learn or there is nothing more to know." When one is genuinely curious, the above statements are considerably different.

1. "You know, although I have been doing this job for a long time, perhaps there are some nuances that I don't fully appreciate or I am not aware of."

2. "My master's degree was very thorough and from an excellent school so reading a profit and loss statement is almost second nature to me. What is it about the profit and loss statement that I might be missing?"

3. "I liked that book so much I read it twice. Your take on the book's point is interesting and not at all what I took away from it. Tell me more about how you understood the author's thinking."

In the second three statements, there is a clear willingness to hear more even though the person might already believe there is nothing more to know. The overt behavior of being curious at the very least sends the message that one open to learning and hearing more. Ideally, there is a genuine curiosity in the person.

LOOKING FOR ORGANIZATIONAL OPPORTUNITIES

Now that you are familiar with mentoring's promise and problems, take a few minutes to think about how to apply mentoring in your organization.

List six ways in which your organization could benefit from formal or informal mentoring. Where is there a need for the benefits that mentoring gives?

1. _____
2. _____
3. _____
4. _____
5. _____
6. _____

Consider how competition, changes in your organization's mission, or other external factors could affect the future of your organization. List six factors that could have an impact on you, your co-workers and the organization as a whole.

1. _____
2. _____
3. _____
4. _____
5. _____
6. _____

In what specific ways could mentoring influence employee development and the organization's future?

_____
_____
_____
_____

MODELING

To model is to display specific behaviors. If they are positive behaviors, then modeling can inspire us to improve ourselves. You probably know people in your organizations that you admire. They could be co-workers or higher-ups.

For each of the following attributes that you may have seen modeled, describe why it is or is not important to you.

1. Integrity _____

_____

2. Sensitivity to others _____

_____

3. Consideration for others _____

_____

4. Moral or ethical leadership _____

_____

5. Loyalty _____

_____

6. Other _____

_____

Who knows? Maybe you are a model for someone and you don't even know it. Perhaps you have characteristics and attributes that others find inspirational and that they admire. What attributes do you think you could bring to a mentoring relationship that you think you model more days than not?

_____

_____

_____

_____

Part Summary

In this part you learned how to use **effective mentoring tools**. You learned how to use **shifting context** and **active listening**. Next, you learned how to **name feelings** and engage in **constructive confrontation**. You learned how to provide information that has **positive impact**. Finally, you learned how to inspire a mentee by **giving permission**.

Fine Tuning & Transitioning the Mentoring Relationship

> "*A telling sign of the quality of a relationship is how the two people behave when it's over.*"
>
> –Anonymous

In this part:

Fine Tuning and Transitioning

As we begin this final part, focus on two specific areas. The first area is that of fine tuning the mentoring relationship. The second and final area is transitioning the relationship when it is over.

Watch Out For Pitfalls

Mentors want good things for their mentees. They want them to be effective, productive, achieving, successful, and happy. However, sometimes with the best of intentions, mentors might encounter some relatively common pitfalls. Watch out for three of these potentially harmful behaviors:

▶ Criticizing

▶ Giving advice

▶ Rescuing people from a self-inflicted folly

Dr. Eric Berne was a psychiatrist best known as the creator of Transaction Analysis and the author of *Games People Play*. He pointed out that the three behaviors listed above are components of psychological games that involve put-downs. These potentially harmful behaviors can impact the mentoring relationship. These behaviors (Dr. Berne called them games) can leave one or both in the mentoring relationship feeling badly.

Criticizing behaviors might begin with an absolute statement such as "John, you are always late, you're never on time." These generalizations trigger rejection of the message, resistance, and argument. So John's actual behavior—the fact that he's late today—is not examined or dealt with. These behaviors tend to become repetitive. The nag continues to nag, the person being nagged resists, and little change in behavior occurs. If left unchecked, this cycle can destroy a relationship.

Most of us have been taught, often by example, to criticize, give advice, and rescue people inappropriately. These behaviors should be substituted with more helpful and healthy behaviors.

The following pages explore each of these behaviors and challenges you to think about productive, effective, and healthy alternatives.

Potential Pitfall One—Giving Criticism

Perhaps it is human nature, perhaps our defense mechanisms kick into high gear, perhaps it's the delivery or maybe all three, but most people do not automatically welcome criticism, even when it is offered as "constructive criticism."

No matter how we sugarcoat it, criticism is by its very nature evaluative and judgmental and from the beginning of this book we have warned against the potential problems of evaluating and judging the mentee. We use the term "constructive criticism" because the inclusion of the word "constructive" implies good intent.

Good intentions can be undercut if criticism is received in a way that damages self-esteem, generates defensive blocking, and drains the energy needed for constructive action. Also, accepting criticism involves acknowledging that a behavior was bad or inappropriate.

Human beings have many internal motivators. Two of the more powerful ones are survival and security. Criticism and evaluation can threaten these motivators. For some people, criticizing, complaining, and nagging tend to prolong the problem and ironically reinforce the behavior.

Avoiding criticism does not mean accepting negative behaviors, performance failures, or self-defeating repetitive actions. When a mentee's behavior is not up to snuff, the mentor must think through an effective intervention.

Do not repeat endlessly and negatively, as critics tend to do, but take new, objective, and creative approaches to encouraging beneficial change. When a person's performance is not up to standard, the person may need information rather than criticism.

Make your point from the other person's perspective. If your approach to giving feedback or constructive criticism is not evidently effective, stop what you are doing and try something else.

Remember to address this potential pitfall as part of your guiding principles.

Healthy Alternatives

What are the "thinking" alternatives to criticism? Mentors are most beneficial when they help their mentees break out of negative behavior patterns. When a person makes the same mistake repeatedly, the solution is not to give the same answer over and over again. The most positive route to change is to look at the transactions and identify the repetitive elements so they can be changed—even if the change is difficult or painful.

For example, if a mentee repeatedly fails when given an assignment, instead of merely encouraging the person to do better, have a "constructive confrontation" to collaboratively analyze what's going on, to be "genuinely curious" together in an effort to find the underlying cause and healthier alternatives.

When someone doesn't do well at something and there is a perception of failure, it can simply be viewed as the gap between what is needed and what was produced. Often the difference between where mentees are and where they're trying to go is tricky to measure. A mutual plan for defining, measuring, and closing the gap can be a helpful tool.

The performance or behavior gap is best described in neutral or factual terms that are specific and measurable. The description can often imply a solution.

EVALUATIVE VS. NEUTRAL TERMS

Think of some personal or performance gaps you have encountered. Describe them first in evaluative terms, then in neutral or factual terms that are specific and measurable.

Evaluative: Your reports are always late.

Neutral/Factual: Your last three reports were each 2 or more days late.

Evaluative: _____

Neutral: _____

Evaluative: _____

Neutral: _____

Evaluative: _____

Neutral: _____

Potential Pitfall Two—Giving Advice

The second pitfall is one that many of us fall into often without knowing it. Giving advice comes naturally for many of us. Many mentors believe that a part of their role is giving advice.

There is a downside to giving advice, because it assumes that the advisor has superior knowledge or insight and that the advice is correct and appropriate. This might or might not be true. It might tend to be more true in a professional setting where the mentor has direct and applicable experience.

However, when the issue is a mentee's personal problem, whether job related or not, the mentor needs to listen very carefully. The mentee might know more about the problem than the mentor does because s/he has been living it. As the mentee talks about his/her issue, listen for patterns, resistance to trying new ways of thinking or acting, blind spots, and contradictions. Advice or suggestions about personal problems can often be met with some level of resistance and the term "yes, but."

A mentor best serves a mentee by:

- ▶ Hearing the person out by using active listening.

- ▶ Feeding back the emotions that are expressed to demonstrate understanding of the deeper, emotional nature of the difficulty. Restating what was heard in a way that the mentee knows the mentor "gets it."

- ▶ Providing ideas or information when asked, which the mentee can use to help weave a solution. The mentor can also ask permission to give ideas or information which, if the relationship is a healthy one, should be welcomed by the mentee.

Whether or not the mentee welcomes ideas and information varies with the person and personalities involved. Mentors should respect mentees' independence and offer ideas but should not push. Mentees must learn to make their own decisions and mentors guide how they learn to do that. Hopefully a mentee values the mentor's experience, ideas, knowledge of how things work, and special insights into problems.

Effective mentors stick with helping, not interfering. They share, they model, they teach; they do not take over someone else's problems unless there is a crisis that requires immediate action. Mentee growth depends on the mentee taking responsibility for solving his or her problems.

Remember, a mentor is a guide.

Information vs. Advice

Psychologist Stephen Karpman devised the Drama Triangle as a way of analyzing psychological games that people play[1]. Dr. Karpman's Drama Triangle describes a three-part relationship between individuals who play the roles of victim, perpetrator, and rescuer. This illustrates why people often resist taking advice. Someone who feels victimized by a problem may plead for help from a person perceived as a rescuer (i.e., a more capable person.) The victim's feelings of inadequacy are real, but the lack of ability usually is not. In a Drama Triangle scenario, the would-be rescuer accepts the inadequacy of the victim and offers advice.

Often the victim rejects the advice with "yes, but," followed by a reason for not taking the advice. This is hardly surprising, since the person knows all of the facts of the problem and has probably already considered and rejected the easy answers.

The rescuer has only the information that the victim gives in response to each suggestion. Each new suggestion is rejected for some seemingly new reason. Sometimes the rescuer grows impatient with the rejections and then can turn persecutor, responding with something to the effect of, "Buzz off—you don't really want to solve this problem."

At that point, both parties are confined to their own judgment. The victim feels even more like a victim—still stuck with the original problem, but now dealing with the frustration of the would-be rescuer. The victim's inadequacy is confirmed in the mind of the rescuer. The victim is convinced that the problem cannot be solved. And the relationship has been damaged.

Here are some possible comments you might hear if you are involved with the Drama Triangle.

► Why don't you/Yes but…

► If it weren't for you…

► Why does this always happen to me?

► See what you made me do?!

► You got me into this!

► Look how hard I have been trying.

► I'm only trying to help you.

Of course, just because you hear these words it doesn't mean you are deep into the triangle. Just consider them to be red flags, or opportunities to be genuinely curious. If these phrases begin to form a pattern, that might be an indicator that a Drama Triangle is at play.

---

[1] Karpman, S. (1968). *Fairy tales and script drama analysis*. Transactional Analysis Bulletin, 7(26), 39–43.

Potential Pitfall Three—Trying to Rescue

The third pitfall is rescuing, in which the mentor takes over a situation because he thinks he has to save someone.

The world has many examples of genuine victims. People who fall on hard times through no fault of their own might include earthquake survivors, auto accident victims, or workers left in the lurch when a business fails. These people need and deserve help.

Another type of victim needs a different type of help. Some individuals set up repetitive patterns of failure. This may be due to feelings of inadequacy, prior victimization, or poor adaptive skills. Many of us do this in some area of our lives. If we never experienced actual failure, we would fail to achieve.

When dysfunctional behavior patterns occur in a mentee's personal or work life, a mentor can help by pointing out the repetitive nature of the transactions. The mentor can use counseling skills to help the mentee break the pattern.

Rescuing the mentee by attempting to take over the problem is helpful in the long run. Temporary help in a crisis might be appropriate, but when there is a recurring pattern of such rescuing, the mentor becomes part of the mentee's problem.

Why might that be? If the mentor continues to rescue or save the mentee, then the mentee will never develop coping, problem solving, and interpersonal skills. The mentee will not be able to stand alone. Once the mentor is gone from the mentee's life, the pattern will repeat with someone else.

There are people whose job it is to rescue people in life-threatening situations like firefighters, doctors, nurses, EMTs, soldiers, police, and lifeguards to name a few. Mentors guide people to find ways of rescuing themselves in non-life threatening situations.

MISDIRECTED HELP

When a mentoring relationship goes off course there is a need for problem identification, definition, and resolution. For each of the following mentee statements, (1) identify the feelings to help define the problem; (2) identify an ineffective intervention or response; and (3) indicate a constructive response.

Sample statement: *"I'm worried about what you told me to do about the Owens situation. If it goes badly my whole career will be up for grabs."*

Feeling: Very scared, possibly angry that his or her career is being discounted.

Ineffective Intervention: "Don't worry about a thing—I wouldn't have suggested it if there was any possibility of it going wrong."

Effective response: "You seem very concerned about the consequences. Let's talk about them in detail. I want to hear exactly what is troubling you."

1. "I think the intern program is a waste of time. It isn't doing me any good and I want to drop out of it."

Feeling: _____

Ineffective intervention: _____

Effective response: _____

2. "Once again I thought I had a chance to really make it, and again I failed."

Feeling: _____

Ineffective intervention: _____

Effective response: _____

3. "It seems as if I can never get ahead. My finances are a mess, I've got bill collectors after me all the time, and I just don't know what to do. I may even have to declare bankruptcy."

Feeling: _____

Ineffective intervention: _____

Effective response: _____

CASE STUDY: Haresh

Haresh Shah recently graduated from a first-class engineering school. He joined your department less than a year ago. He is amiable and well liked by his co-workers. His engineering qualifications are impressive.

You are Lee Backus, his technical supervisor. You are the lead designer and have been with the organization for 12 years. You spent considerable time teaching Haresh as much as you could, but there is a language barrier. You have a hard time understanding his speech and he sometimes seems to have trouble understanding yours.

Haresh's family emigrated here several years ago. Relatives sponsored his family in the United States, and Haresh completed most of high school and college here with good marks.

By working very hard at it, Haresh can adequately present his ideas in writing, but his verbal presentations are not clear. It is hard to follow his syntax and understand his words. His presentation to an in-house weekly symposium went poorly. His slides were loaded with equations, he mumbled as he read notes, remained behind the podium, failed to look at his audience, and he presented his verbal information in a sketchy, abbreviated fashion.

Some participants dozed, some read other materials, and a few talked among themselves. During the question-and-answer period, not one question was raised. You were embarrassed by Haresh and by your colleagues' behavior.

After the presentation, you met with Haresh to debrief on the presentation. You shared your impressions of how it went and Haresh seemed crest-fallen. He said that he put in long hours to make the presentation as effective as it was. His body language and his tone seemed to indicate that his self-esteem and confidence had just taken a severe hit.

Later your manager took you aside to get your evaluation of Haresh's presentation. Once you told him, he then asked you to mentor Haresh as well as supervise him. Since you were teaching him the work as fast and as well as you could, you thought you had been mentoring. When you pointed this out, your boss said, "No, this goes beyond doing your job. Try to be a friend to him, help him to succeed. Do what you can to turn him into a winner."

CONTINUED

CONTINUED

Helping Haresh

1. List some possible obstacles to Haresh's success.

_____

_____

_____

2. What cross-cultural elements might come into play in this situation?

_____

_____

_____

3. List some ideas for helping Haresh.

_____

_____

_____

Compare your answers to those of the author in the Appendix.

" *There are two primary choices in life: to accept conditions as they exist, or accept responsibility for changing them."*

–Denis Waitley

CASE STUDY: Mary Jane

Mary Jane is 72 and hasn't missed a day of work in more than 30 years. She is cheerful and helpful to everyone, performs well, and says she expects to be around until she's a 110. Mary Jane thrives on hard work. She participates in civic and charitable activities and takes one college course a semester—usually on a professional subject, but occasionally she signs up for a "fun course." Pictures of her grandchildren and great-grandchildren adorn her office.

Recently, Ellen Kuhary announced she will retire in seven months. The next day Mary Jane asked you to help her prepare to apply for Ellen's job. She is amply qualified and has the seniority—though seniority here is more a custom than a rule. She noted that you have successfully mentored several women, and though you are not in Ellen's chain-of-command you know a lot about her work that would be helpful.

You are a corporate vice president, the most successful woman in the corporation. You have broken many historical taboos about women's careers. You could provide unique insight into Ellen's job and its relationship to the work of other departments. However, Kurt Smith, Ellen's supervisor, doesn't take kindly to other people's involvement in his area.

Mary Jane told Kurt she is interested in Ellen's job. He was surprised and commented on her age. She shot back that his remark could be the basis of an age-discrimination suit, but that she wanted to win the job by her proven ability and her record. She reportedly left Kurt gasping for breath. The Federal Age Discrimination in Employment Act and a state law allow Mary Jane to continue working indefinitely, as long as her performance meets standards.

Mary Jane also told Ellen she wanted to be her successor. She said, "Succeeding in your job would be the crowning feather in my career cap." Ellen likes Mary Jane and is probably mentoring her in some informal, unofficial capacity. However, Mary Jane has told you clearly that she wants to "earn that job."

CONTINUED

In light of the politics, what are the factors involved with your mentoring Mary Jane?

_____

_____

_____

List as many things that you think you would be able to offer Mary Jane if you were to be her mentor.

_____

_____

_____

_____

Create a list of possible guiding principles for your mentoring relationship with Mary Jane.

_____

_____

_____

_____

Identify the various elements that should be part of a mentoring agreement you might make with Mary Jane.

_____

_____

_____

What personal rewards might you derive from mentoring Mary Jane?

_____

_____

_____

Mary Jane is a treasure to her organization. Based on her performance, she could continue to add considerable value to the organization for many years to come.

If you are her mentor you should explore your own attitudes, beliefs, and possibly stereotypes about her age, health, and personal contributions on the job. To what degree do any of your own attitudes affect your ability positively or negatively to mentor Mary Jane?

People who are more fully developed than others through their life experiences, education, and general temperament tend not to be shackled by stereotypes. They are quite often well suited to relate well to other people who fall outside our traditional concepts of the ideal employee, such as the physically or mentally challenged, the bias against older employees which is fairly common, and all of the other differences that sometimes block fairness toward an individual.

The challenge has been for decades now to use all types of diversity to benefit your organization. Each human being is incredibly complex and brings a whole myriad of talents and skills as well as potential challenges when it comes to "fitting in."

Mary Jane is a clear example of the increasingly common phenomenon of a person who loves her involvement in her work, her community, and the finely woven web of relationships that are built over years. If it seems strange to have a particular kind of mentee such as older or from another culture or not from your department, quite possibly there will be a lot for you to learn. May you step outside of your "normal zone" and be as open as possible to the learning waiting for you and your mentee.

"Being my mentee does not guarantee you'll eventually be as cool as me."

Transitioning the Relationship

Rarely do healthy mentoring relationships end. The ties that are created during the highs and lows of shared mentoring tend to bond the two people for a lifetime.

When I was in my early twenties, I was mentored by a blind man. This blind man taught everything he could about taking apart grand pianos and putting them back together with care and precision. For two years he was my mentor. Decades have passed. To this day, that bond of guidance, mutual respect, and deep gratitude is as strong as it was back then.

Because a good mentoring experience has such deep impact on those involved, the relationship usually doesn't end; it transitions to a different kind of relationship. Sometimes a mentee becomes a peer of his/her mentor. Sometimes mentees actually become a former mentor's manager. Regardless of scenario, it is very important to transition the mentoring relationship mindfully and respectfully to give it closure.

During the first stage of the relationship (the forming stage), it is useful to talk about this last stage (the adjourn stage.) Having the foresight to do this can improve the eventual transitioning.

Meet with the specific purpose of transitioning the relationship. Discussing the following provides a wealth of benefits.

▶ Reflect on the overall process. What was it like for both parties?

▶ What were the highlights?

▶ What were the challenges and how did we handle them?

▶ What did we learn that is actionable? What will we do differently going forward?

▶ What kind of relationship would we like to have now that this part of the relationship is over?

▶ How shall we celebrate our accomplishment?

Hopefully each person will think of things to say to express their appreciation for what each of them has gained from the mentoring relationship.

TRANSITIONING THE MENTORING RELATIONSHIP

Imagine that you are in the process of officially ending a mentoring relationship. Now that the mentoring relationship is coming to a close, what kinds of things do you think the mentor and mentee need to say to each other?

_____

_____

_____

If the relationship is to continue, what might that look like—now that mentoring is no longer in the picture?

_____

_____

_____

What are some specific things that the mentor and mentee should do to transition the relationship?

_____

_____

_____

What are some ways the mentor and mentee can celebrate this transition or adjournment?

_____

_____

_____

Remember to be sure to give the mentoring relationship the kind of transition that it deserves.

Part Summary

In this part, you learned how to **fine-tune** and **transition** the mentoring relationship. You learned how to avoid three **pitfalls**: giving **criticism**, giving **advice**, and trying to **rescue**. Finally, you learned how to **transition** a relationship once mentoring has officially come to a halt.

A P P E N D I X

Appendix to Part 2

Comments & Suggested Responses

Case Study: Gen and Manuel

1. What career opportunities might exist in this scenario?

    Gen sounds like an ideal individual to take a reverse mentoring role. She has a wide range of skills and some global experience that Manuel might learn from.

    Manuel is nearly a generation older and has been at the company longer. He might be able to mentor Gen in terms of understanding corporate culture, avoiding political landmines, and networking with co-workers.

2. If Manuel decided to pursue these opportunities, how might he go about it?

    If Manuel felt comfortable doing so, he might approach Gen directly, and suggest an informal, short-term, reverse mentoring relationship.

    Because both Manuel and Gen report to the same superior, Manuel could suggest the mentoring idea to the boss. If their superior brokers the relationship, then it is likely to be more highly structured.

3. What are some possible challenges or issues?

    Gen is considerably younger than Manuel. In addition to being younger, Gen has been at the company for a much shorter time than Manuel. One or both of them might feel uncomfortable with the concept of a "younger teaching older" relationship.

    Both Gen and Manuel come from cultural backgrounds in which women are encouraged to be subservient to men. One or both of them might feel uncomfortable with the concept of cross-gender mentoring.

    U.S. corporate culture is not immune to machismo issues. Manuel should consider the reaction his peers and superiors might have when they learn he is being mentored by a younger female with little time on the job.

    Both Gen and Manuel are living and working in a culture that is different from the one in which they were raised. Adapting to a new culture no doubt presented challenges for each of them. If they enter into a mentoring relationship, both will now have to learn and adapt to a third culture (the other person's.) One or both of them might feel uncomfortable with the concept of cross-cultural mentoring.

If both Gen and Manuel are open to the idea of a reverse mentoring relationship, they should discuss these issues thoroughly, to ensure that their interests and expectations are aligned.

4. Who within the company might be able to help Manuel pursue these opportunities?

   Manuel works with a vice president to whom he does not report. In addition to their direct superior, Manuel might be able to get the vice president of the Chicago district office to use his influence to help Manuel pursue this opportunity.

Considerations for this scenario:

▶ In what specific ways can Manuel help Gen?

▶ In what specific ways can Gen help Manuel?

▶ How can Manuel bring out more of Gen's talents in a way that adds value for Gen and for the company? Is it even Manuel's job to do this? Why should he?

▶ How could both of them add value to the company in operational and strategic arenas?

Appendix to Part 3

Comments & Suggested Responses

Paula

1. If you decide to continue informally mentoring Paula, what special aspects of mentoring would you emphasize?

   You could emphasize personal growth and career development.

2. Would your mentoring be affected if you were a male? How?

   If the mentor is a male, then both parties need to discuss the benefits and pitfalls of cross-gender mentoring.

3. How would you attempt to make Paula more aware of her special abilities and talents?

   You might arrange for Paula to be assigned to projects or teams that would allow her to display her gifts.

4. How would you convey to her the importance of speaking positively about herself?

   You could suggest specific books to Paula that would help her to overcome her habit of talking herself down. In conversation, you could call her on it every time it happens.

5. In what specific ways could you help Paula?

   You could suggest books or training courses to help Paula with her self-image issues. If you know Harold Greening, you might suggest to him that Paula is ready to take on bigger challenges. You could tell Paula to look at job postings within the company to try to advance her career.

Appendix to Part 4

Comments & Suggested Responses

Ray

Perhaps when you and Ray began your mentoring relationship, more time should have been spent on setting ground rules. Proactive talks about specific behaviors might have helped Ray behave better, especially if there had been constructive confrontation along the way to guide him.

Certainly Ray has many qualities that could make him a valuable employee. You might be able to help him yet. Here are some suggested answers to the questions in the exercise.

1. Begin by asking Ray what position he hopes to achieve in the company—next year, five years from now, ten years from now. Ask him to name some people who already hold those positions. Ask how he thinks they achieved their positions. Ask about his perceptions of their behavior now, and ask how that behavior might have changed after they received promotions. Doing this might make Ray begin to question if he is modeling behavior that leads to success in your company.

2. Ray seems to see managers (including his superior) as obstacles to his own success. His performance on work assigned by his superior seems to indicate the he does not take his superior seriously and that he does not see job performance as a path to success. By focusing on making connections, it seems he believes that success is tied to "who you know."

3. Begin by asking Ray if he is willing to discuss what could be a touchy subject—your observation of his behavior

   Start with a neutral, factual, or unbiased "description" of his behavior, such as "I have heard you refer to your supervisor's assignments as 'busy work.'" By doing this you reflect back to Ray what you have heard him say. You could follow this by saying, "Ray, if you were a co-worker and you heard this, what would you think about you?" Based on his answers you might let him know that his supervisor describes his efforts as "hastily performed, somewhat sloppy work."

   Next you could ask Ray what negative effects his behavior might have on co-workers or his supervisor. Remind Ray gently that it his supervisor who writes his performance appraisals.

Then ask Ray if you can share with him some of your reactions (feeling and thoughts) about the impact this observed behavior is having on Ray and others.

Be kind if you can; you *must* be honest. "Ray, you know that I care about you and I want you to succeed. But I also care about this organization. As your mentor and as a co-worker, I am troubled by your behavior."

Do not tell Ray how to behave—he must decide this on his own. Do not threaten or pressure him—that will enable him to justify resistance. Help him to understand that how he chooses to be perceived will be the deciding factor in things like his performance reviews, promotions, and friendships. Help him to understand that this *is* a choice and that he is largely responsible for how he is perceived.

Appendix to Part 5

Comments & Suggested Responses

Haresh

Your supervisor is asking you to rise above the level supervisor, teacher, and coach and add the extra dimension of mentor to the relationship. To be a "friend," to "help him succeed," to "do what you can to turn him into a winner." These are all challenging goals with potentially great rewards.

There is a gap between Haresh's current performance level and his needed performance level. Your conversation with him should focus on this gap

Be cautious regarding your manager's directive to *"Try to be a friend to him, help him to succeed. Do what you can to turn him into a winner."* These multiple roles could be difficult to juggle. Being Haresh's mentor, supervisor, and friend can present a whole host of conflicting role dynamics. Go cautiously down those parallel roads. Be very sure to create clear and defined boundaries so that Haresh is not confused by the three-part role you are being asked to play.

1. Some possible obstacles to Haresh's success include:

    a. Poor spoken English skills

    b. Poor presentation delivery skills (e.g., mumbling, remaining behind the podium)

    c. Poor presentation design skills (slides filled with formulae)

    d. Low self-confidence

2. Cross-cultural elements that might come into play include the language barrier, and any expectations that Haresh might have concerning how he should be perceived due to his engineering skills. His tendency to mumble and avoid eye contact might be a cultural habit intended to avoid calling attention to oneself.

3. Some ideas for helping Haresh might include:

   a. Suggest to Haresh that he enroll in English as a Second Language classes. Since he already attended high school and college in the United States, he should find an advanced class the focuses on polishing his skills. This will give Haresh specific instruction on any shortcomings and also the practice he needs to become fluent. Classes might be offered by a local community college or other institution. You could suggest to your manager that the company offer to pay for the classes.

   b. There are a number of things you might do to help improve Haresh's delivery:

      i. Send him to a one- or two-day class on presentation delivery skills—how to dynamically engage an audience.

      ii. Have Haresh give one or more brief presentations to two people in a small room. No slides.

      iii. As his mentor, review and critique every presentation Haresh prepares—before he gives it.

   c. Suggest to Haresh any of several books on designing effective presentation slides. These are available in great numbers from any online book store.

   d. To build Haresh's confidence, remind him during coaching sessions of the contribution he makes through his impressive engineering skills. Compliment him on the progress he makes in improving his English skills and his presentations. Your manager wants you to turn Haresh into a winner. Tell him you think he already is a winner.

CRiSP

50-Minute™ Series

If you enjoyed this book, we have great news for you.
There are more than 200 books available in the
Crisp Fifty-Minute™ Series.

Subject Areas Include:

Management and Leadership
Human Resources
Communication Skills
Personal Development
Sales and Marketing
Accounting and Finance
Coaching and Mentoring
Customer Service/Quality
Small Business and Entrepreneurship
Writing and Editing

For more information visit us online at

www.CrispSeries.com

AXZO PRESS